Withdra

D1588873

HOUSEHOLD INSECT PESTS

THE RENTOKIL LIBRARY

The Woodworm Problem
The Dry Rot Problem
Household Insect Pests

TITLES IN PREPARATION

The Cockroach
Stored Products Entomology
Rodents and Hygiene
The Termite Problem

THE RENTOKIL LIBRARY

HOUSEHOLD INSECT PESTS

*An outline of the identification, biology
and control of the common insect pests
found in the home*

NORMAN E. HICKIN

*Scientific Director
Rentokil Laboratories Limited*

HUTCHINSON OF LONDON

HUTCHINSON & CO. (*Publishers*) LTD.
178–202 Great Portland Street, London W.1

London   Melbourne   Sydney
Auckland   Bombay   Toronto
Johannesburg   New York

First published 1964

*Printed in Great Britain by Benham and Company Limited, Colchester
and bound by William Brendon and Son Limited, in Tiptree, Essex*

CONTENTS

Acknowledgements   *page*   7

Introduction   9

List of Colour Plates   11

List of species mentioned in the text   13

Part I

1. WHAT IS AN INSECT?   17
How insects and mites are identified from other animals—Why are some insects
found indoors?—Fortuitous introductions and wanderers from the garden

2. THE ANATOMY AND EVOLUTION OF AN INSECT   21
The life-cycle of an insect—How insects grow—How insects evolved and how
they are classified—How insects are named

Part II

3. SILVERFISH AND SPRINGTAILS   43
Thysanura and *Collembola*

4. THE COCKROACHES, CRICKET AND EARWIG   47
Dictyoptera, *Orthoptera* and *Dermaptera*

5. LICE   56
Book Louse, Head and Body Lice and Dog Lice
Psocoptera, *Mallophaga* and *Anoplura*

6. THE BED BUG   64
Hemiptera—Heteroptera

7. LACEWINGS AND MOTHS   67
Green Lacewing, Clothes and House Moths
Neuroptera and *Lepidoptera*

8. BEETLES   75
Wood-boring Beetles—Mealworm Beetle—Spider Beetles—Plaster Beetles—
Larder Beetle—Carpet Beetles and other beetles
Coleoptera

9. WASPS AND ANTS   105
Hymenoptera

10. FLIES AND GNATS   113
    Cluster Fly—Window Gnat—House Fly—Seaweed Fly—Fruit Fly—
    Mosquitoes and other two-winged flies
    Diptera

11. HUMAN, CAT AND DOG FLEAS   132
    Siphonaptera

12. THE WOOD LOUSE AND CENTIPEDE   137
    Some non-insect pests

13. MITES AND TICKS   141
    Furniture Mites—Flour Mites—Scabies (itch) Mites—Sheep Ticks
    Acari

Part III

14. NOTES ON CONTROL   153

Bibliography   166

Index   167

ACKNOWLEDGEMENTS

I must acknowledge the help generously given to me by my colleagues on the staff of Rentokil Research Laboratories. Mr. R. K. Farmer, the Laboratory Controller, allowed me to use his notes for a manual of insect pests. Many of the photographs are the work of the Laboratory's Photographic Unit. I am very grateful to Mr. Robin Edwards who painstakingly corrected the typescripts and proofs and made many suggestions. Lastly, I wish to thank Mrs. Rhona Priddey for her valuable contribution. In spite of the many calls on her time she provided the secretarial services for the first drafts, often at short notice. This book first appeared as a weekly supplement to the *Rentokil Recorder* edited by my old friend and colleague Mr. W. M. Sproat.

INTRODUCTION

All animals have associated with them a number of insects and other small creatures which are either parasitic on them or dependent on them in one way or another as scavengers or for shelter. Man is no exception. Indeed, as man evolved from his primitive state, he utilized branches of trees for his dwellings and skin and fur for his clothing, and he stored food against the winter. In so doing, he brought innumerable small animals into his home. It has been rightly said that man has created his own pests, and it can be appreciated that quite apart from the parasitic insects that live on him and suck his blood, he is host to a veritable stream of insects and other related small animals that quite naturally feed on, and thus decay the dead organic matter that he employs, be it stored grain, wood or fur and feather. The parasites of his domestic animals swell the numbers.

In addition, many insects living precariously on the fringe of their distribution in temperate regions find shelter in man's immediate environment, safe either from the dessicating wind or the mould-laden dampness of the British winter.

Perhaps it is because a number of insects sting or bite, that man has a detestation for insect life, (with the exception of the Honey Bee that he has domesticated). This detestation is something much more than the economic loss which he suffers, although no doubt in more primitive times heavy infestation of stored foods during the winter months could bring starvation and death.

Today, the degree of freedom from insect pests in the home is one of the criteria of the standard of living which is enjoyed. The highest standards are those in which no insect pests of any description, and the consequent anxieties produced, are allowed to intrude into the home.

Insects have adapted themselves to a far wider range of habitats than have any other group of animals. They are ubiquitous. In number of different species, the class INSECTA outnumbers all the other classes of animals added together. It is not surprising, therefore, to find that a relatively large number of insects have successfully adapted themselves to man's economy, and even today, when personal and domestic hygiene is paramount, many species are increasing in numbers. It will be seen, then, that domestic insect pests fall into several groups: those that are parasites on the person, generally blood-suckers such as the Body Louse and Bed Bug; those that infest food, reducing it in quantity and fouling it, such as the Cockroach; and those that infest clothes and furnishings made of wool or of other material of animal origin, such as the Clothes Moths and Carpet

Beetles. In yet another group they infest wood in various forms, furniture and structural timber of housing. The immature stage of these insects is known as woodworm.

Lastly, there occurs a group of insects found in the home which appear to do little or no damage, but naturally the housewife does not like to see them about. These are the nuisance insects.

As the life-cycles and general habits of these insect pests differ one from another, obviously the first stage in eliminating them from the home is to know something about them and to be able to identify them correctly, so that appropriate measures can be taken against them. The aim of this little book is to help in identification, to give a summary of the biology, and some notes on extermination, and it contains four coloured plates and a number of line-drawings depicting all the more common insect pests which may be found in the home. The essential prelude to the successful extermination of any of these disquieting animals is correct identification, and we believe that the book has made this task as simple as possible. Indeed, we think that any householder will now be able to identify these pests with exactitude.

Many of what can be called the 'social' pests, such as the Head Louse and Bed Bug, are happily on the decline, but even so they often turn up in homes due to inexplicable causes, and prompt measures are necessary for early extermination. On the other hand, some pests in the home are at the present time increasing rapidly, an example being the Common Furniture Beetle.

The text-matter includes not only descriptions of the adult insects but also reference to the immature stages, and it is divided into two parts. General information about insects is given in Part I so that the detailed information concerning 74 insects (and their near relations) can be more readily understood. Part II contains detailed information concerning the individual species.

The housewife often gets very worried when insects turn up in numbers in the home, but often she is at a loss to know where to turn for information. This book will enable her to identify the pests in the vast majority of cases, and if further detailed information is required the list of specialized books given in the bibliography, and the list of addresses where further help may be obtained, will supply it.

LIST OF COLOUR PLATES

PLATE I

Silverfish
German Cockroach

House Cricket
Bed Bug

PLATE II

Brown House Moth
Common Clothes Moth

White-Shouldered House Moth
Larva of Case-bearing Clothes Moth

Case-bearing Clothes Moth

PLATE III

Common Furniture Beetle
Fur Beetle

Powder Post Beetle
Mealworm Beetle

PLATE IV

Australian Spider Beetle
Hump Spider Beetle

Golden Spider Beetle
Bread Beetle

Opposite pages 80, 81, 96 and 97

11

LIST OF SPECIES OF INSECTS AND OTHER ARTHROPODS DEALT WITH IN THE TEXT

Note: This list also includes common insects which can be said to be innocuous or beneficial.

Insecta	Order	Common Name	Scientific Name
APTERYGOTA	THYSANURA	Silverfish	*Lepisma saccharina*
		Firebrat	*Thermobia domestica*
	COLLEMBOLA	Springtail	
EXOPTERYGOTA	DICTYOPTERA	German Cockroach	*Blattella germanica*
		Oriental Cockroach	*Blatta orientalis*
	ORTHOPTERA	House Cricket	*Gryllulus domesticus*
	DERMAPTERA	Earwig	*Forficula auricularia*
	PSOCOPTERA	Book-Louse	*Liposcelis divinatorius*
	MALLOPHAGA	Dog Biting Louse	*Trichodectes canis*
	ANOPLURA	Head Louse	*Pediculus humanus capitis*
		Body Louse	*Pediculus humanus corporis*
		Dog Louse	*Linognathus setosus*
		Crab Louse	*Phthirus pubis*
	HEMIPTERA	Bed Bug	*Cimex lectularius*
ENDOPTERYGOTA	NEUROPTERA	Green Lacewing Fly	*Chrysopa carnea*
	LEPIDOPTERA	Common Clothes Moth	*Tineola bisselliella*
		Case Bearing Clothes Moth	*Tinaea pellionella*
		Tapestry Moth	*Trichophaga tapetzella*
		Brown House Moth	*Hofmannophila pseudospretella*
		White-Shouldered House Moth	*Endrosis sarcitrella*
	COLEOPTERA	Common Furniture Beetle	*Anobium punctatum*
		Death Watch Beetle	*Xestobium rufovillosum*
		Weevil (Wood-boring) {	*Euophryum confine* / *Pentarthrum huttoni*
		House Longhorn Beetle	*Hylotrupes bajulus*
		Powder Post Beetle	*Lyctus brunneus*
		Wharf Borer	*Nacerdes melanura*
		Bread Beetle	*Stegobium paniceum*
		Mealworm	*Tenebrio molitor*
		Australian Spider Beetle	*Ptinus tectus*
		Golden Spider Beetle	*Niptus hololeucus*
		Hump Spider Beetle	*Gibbium psylloides*
		Larder Beetle	*Dermestes lardarius*
		Varied Carpet Beetle	*Anthrenus verbasci*
		Fur Beetle	*Attagenus pellio*
		Ladybird Beetle	*COCCINELLIDAE*
		Ground Beetle	*CARABIDAE*

Insecta	Order	Common Name	Scientific Name
		Plaster Beetle	$\left\{\begin{array}{l}\textit{Cryptophagus} \text{ spp.} \\ \textit{Enicmus minutus} \\ \textit{Lathridius bergrothi} \\ \textit{Coninomus nodifer}\end{array}\right.$
		Garden Weevil	*Otiorrhynchus* spp.
	HYMENOPTERA	Common Wasp	*Paravespula vulgaris*
		German Wasp	*Paravespula germanica*
		Pharaoh's Ant	*Monomorium pharaonis*
		Black Garden Ant	*Lasius* (*Acanthomyops*) *niger*
	DIPTERA	Seaweed Fly	*Coelopa frigida*
		Cluster Fly	*Pollenia rudis*
		Window Gnat	*Anisopus fenestralis*
		Yellow Swarming Fly	*Thaumatomyia notata*
		House Fly	*Musca domestica*
		Lesser House Fly	*Fannia canicularis*
		Blue Bottle	*Calliphora erythro-cephala*
		Fruit-Fly	*Drosophilla* spp.
		Green Cluster Fly	*Dasyphora cyanella*
		Crane-Fly	*TIPULIDAE*
		Mosquito	$\left\{\begin{array}{l}\textit{Anopheles maculipennis} \\ \textit{Anopheles atroparvus} \\ \textit{Taeniorhynchus} \\ \quad \textit{richiardii} \\ \textit{Culex pipiens} \\ \textit{Theobaldia annulata}\end{array}\right.$
	SIPHONAPTERA	Human Flea	*Pulex irritans*
		Cat Flea	*Ctenocephalides felis*
		Dog Flea	*Ctenocephalides canis*
CRUSTACEA	ISOPODA	Wood Louse	$\left\{\begin{array}{l}\textit{Oniscus asellus} \\ \textit{Porcellio scaber} \\ \textit{Armadillidium vulgare}\end{array}\right.$
CHILOPODA		Centipede	$\left\{\begin{array}{l}\textit{Necrophlaeophagus} \\ \quad \textit{longicornis} \\ \textit{Lithobius forficatus}\end{array}\right.$
ARACHNIDA	ACARI	Furniture Mite	*Glycyphagus domesticus*
		Flour Mite	*Acarus siro*
		Scabies (itch) Mite	*Sarcoptes scabiei*
		Harvest Mite	*Trombicula autumnalis*
		Red Spider Mite	*Bryobia* spp.
		Grain Itch Mite	*Pyemotes ventricosus*
		Sheep Tick	*Ixodes ricinus*

Part I

1

WHAT IS AN INSECT?

How insects and mites are identified from other animals—Why are some insects found indoors?—Fortuitous introductions and wanderers from the garden

Insects are animals of the class INSECTA which in turn belong to the large group or *phylum* ARTHROPODA. All members of the group ARTHROPODA have the body divided into segments and the skeleton consists of a hard or horny external covering. This is known as an exo-skeleton. In addition, a number of the body segments bear pairs of appendages which are jointed and which vary in size and shape according to their function and to their position on the body.

The group INSECTA, or Insects, consists of arthropods in which, in the adult stage, the body is divided into three distinct regions:

The head   which bears a single pair of antennae, a pair of mandibles and two pairs of mouth parts called maxillae, the second pair of which is fused down the centre.

The thorax   from which arises three pairs of legs and either one or two pairs of wings. In the more primitive insects, however, wings have not been evolved, e.g. the Silverfish *Lepisma saccharina*, and in some highly evolved insects the wings have been lost, e.g. the fleas, SIPHONAPTERA.

The abdomen which bears neither walking legs nor wings but a genital opening occurs near the extremity.

Insects may also be differentiated anatomically by their method of breathing. Air is circulated to all regions and organs of the body through a ramification of minute tubes called trachaea (the smallest are called tracheoles) which open to the outside through pores or spiracles situated along the sides of the body.

How are insects and mites identified from other animals? As already stated, insects are jointed animals, which in the adult stage have the body divided into three distinct regions, the middle region bearing six legs, and usually either one or two pairs of wings in addition. Let us, however, examine some of the other main groups or 'classes' in the ARTHROPODA.

THE CRUSTACEA: This group contains animals of very diverse appearance but Crabs, Shrimps, Lobsters and Wood Lice are well-known examples. The majority of the CRUSTACEA are aquatic, either marine or freshwater, but the Wood Louse is terrestrial.

B   17

THE ARACHNIDA: This group contains the Spiders, Scorpions, Mites and Ticks. They are characterized by the body usually being divided into two distinct parts, the cephalothorax and abdomen. There are four pairs of legs in the adult stage, all arising from the first-named part. There are no antennae. Many immature forms bear only six legs so that the number of legs is not always a reliable guide. In the Harvestmen, PHALANGIIDAE, the cephalothorax and abdomen are so fused that only one part of the body is discernible. Mites are placed in the ARACHNIDA. They possess eight legs in the adult stage but six only when immature. The body is not divided into distinct parts, being sac-like. Six-legged mite larvae can thus be identified from insects by this latter character. Mites are always very small in size.

THE CHILOPODA: These are the centipedes. Each segment typically bears one pair of walking legs but the first pair are modified to form poison claws.

THE DIPLOPODA: This group consists of the millipedes. Each apparent segment of the body bears two pairs of legs. Millipedes have the ability to coil up like a watch-spring if disturbed.

The two classes CHILOPODA and DIPLOPODA, together with some rarer groups, are sometimes placed together in one class called the MYRIAPODA.

Why are some insects found indoors? The insects found in our homes can be divided into a number of categories, as follows:

I. Firstly, those that are direct parasites of man and suck his blood, e.g. the Bed Bug (*Cimex lectularius*), the Human Flea (*Pulex irritans*), the Body Louse (*Pediculus humanus*) and the Scabies or Itch Mite (*Sarcoptes scabiei*). All these creatures have a very close association with man, and therefore may be brought into the home by close human contact or by contact with infested clothing or bedding. Domestic animals such as cats and dogs commonly bear parasitic insects and mites such as fleas and lice of characteristic species. In this respect, man is not different from most other warm-blooded animals in that the latter carry or are closely associated with a number of specific blood-sucking parasites.

II. In this group are included those insects in the adult stage that suck blood, such as the blood-sucking flies, but whose larvae obtain nourishment elsewhere. As an example, the mosquito *Anopheles maculipennis* lays its eggs in standing water and the larvae live on minute aquatic organisms. In many parts of the world, blood-sucking flies are of great medical importance in that they transmit disease, by carrying organisms in the blood, from one host to another.

III. Those insects whose larvae obtain their nourishment from human or domestic animal faecal matter or from waste or discarded meat. The adult stage of these insects, for example the House Fly (*Musca domestica*) and the Lesser House Fly (*Fannia canicularis*), are attracted to buildings where humans and domestic animals are to be found. They are a hazard to health because of the pathogenic organisms that may be carried by them from faecal matter to food.

IV. The insects and mites of this group are found in human habitation because they, or more usually their larvae, subsist on stored foodstuffs of various sorts. This group is sometimes divided into two:

(a) Those that live and breed in the house structure and visit the stored foodstuffs to feed. Examples are the Cockroaches, (*Blattella germanica* and *Blatta orientalis*), the Cricket (*Gryllullus domesticus*), and Ants (*Monomorium pharaonis* and *Lasius niger*).

(b) Those that both live and breed in the foodstuffs, in some cases only making short flights for mating. Examples of this group are Bread Beetle (*Stegobium paniceum*), Larder Beetle (*Dermestes lardarius*), Australian Spider Beetle (*Ptinus tectus*) and the Flour Mite (*Acarus siro*).

V. Next should be considered those insects which feed on organic matter, and because man utilizes such material in his home, these insects find their way indoors and feed on the same materials. They can be conveniently divided into two groups as follows:

(a) Those insects that subsist on fur, feathers, skin and wool. These are Clothes Moths and House Moths (*Tineola bisselliella* and *Hofmannophila pseudospretella*) and the Carpet and Fur Beeltes (*Anthrenus verbasci* and *Attagenus pellio*). Outside man's economy these insects are found where there are accumulations of fur and feathers, such as in old birds'-nests.

(b) Those insects whose larvae bore into wood and are able to subsist on wood maintained under the conditions present in buildings. These insects are given the general name of Woodworm and examples are the Common Furniture Beetle (*Anobium punctatum*) and the Powder Post Beetle (*Lyctus brunneus*). All wood-boring insects found in buildings are also to be found out of doors infesting dead or dying trunks and branches of trees, but not always in the same country where they are pests indoors.

VI. *Fortuitous introductions and wanderers from the garden.* This last group is a very large one and consists of insects, mites, an isopod crustacean (the Wood Louse, *Oniscus*, etc.) and occasionally centipedes and millipedes which wander into your homes by accident, although the actual attraction which directs them indoors varies. Some species, and perhaps the majority come into this category, are attracted to light and enter through open windows on summer evenings. Next morning they are found by the housewife who wonders what they are doing in her home. Many moths and beetles fly into buildings for this reason.

Some insects wander into houses because they naturally seek cracks, crevices and stones in or under which they can hide during daylight hours. Many carabid beetles which are beneficial garden insects creep under the kitchen door and hide under the mat where, alas, they are killed.

A small group of insects enter buildings because they are seeking a place for hibernation and come into an open window in the autumn perhaps mistaking it for a hollow tree. The Small Tortoiseshell Butterfly is a well-known hibernator in our homes but the Lacewing Fly (*Chysopa carnea*) and the Ladybird Beetle (COCCINELLIDAE) also enter for shelter.

Lastly, mention must be made of insects and mites which come into our buildings quite fortuitously, in fact just as though the building was part of the garden. A good example of this is the Red Spider Mite (*Bryobia* spp.) which often occurs in such large numbers in the garden that they will spill over and climb up the wall, through the open window and into a room.

2

THE ANATOMY AND EVOLUTION
OF AN INSECT

The life-cycle of an insect—How insects grow—How insects evolved and how they are classified—How insects are named

Because insects vary so much not only in their external appearance but in their internal anatomy, it is usual to refer to a hypothetical insect for a general account, and the reader's attention is directed to Fig. 1 in this regard.

The horny external skeleton of an insect is divided into a number of hard immovable plates, either shield-shaped, such as on top of or below the various segments of the abdomen, or they may be cylindrical, such as on the various parts of the legs.

Each hard inelastic part, however, is joined to adjacent parts by a thin movable elastic membrane. Each of these parts, in entomological textbooks, is given a definite name, so that the part in one insect can be compared with the similar part in another insect.

The exoskeleton, or main integument, then, by the shape of its separate units produces the three main characteristic parts of the insect—head, thorax and abdomen, as shown in Fig. 1. The relation of the blood system, the alimentary canal, the nervous system and reproductive system to the integument is also shown.

The Blood or Vascular System

In an insect, circulation of blood takes place in open cavities of the body system which includes also cavities in all the appendages, such as legs and antennae. There is only one closed blood-vessel. This consists of a long tube known as the dorsal vessel which lies immediately beneath the integument at the top or dorsal surface of the insect in the middle line. The front part, which commences behind the brain and traverses the thorax, is thin, and is called the aorta. The hinder part which traverses the whole of the abdomen is segmented in relation to the segments of the abdomen and is wider than the aorta and is known as the heart. In each segment is a pair of slit-like openings which allows blood to enter and is there pumped forwards to the aorta which is the main artery.

The blood of insects consists of liquid plasma and blood-cells or haemocytes. It freely bathes the internal organs and appendages. The blood-cells store and transport food substances and the plasma is the main storage of water. The blood also carries hormones around the body and also has a mechanical function in such actions as expansion of wings as, for example, in butterflies and moth. It should be noted that in the blood of insects the transport of oxygen is of relatively little importance, on account of the extensive and efficient development of the tracheal system.

The Alimentary Canal

The alimentary canal of insects is a fairly simple tube having its origin at the mouth and ending at the anus at the hinder end of the abdomen. The alimentary canal of the Cockroach is shown in Fig. 2. In some insects it is straight but in others it is long enough to be thrown into a series of folds. The alimentary canal is divided into three main parts according to its embryonic origin.

The fore intestine: This originates as a pushing-in of the integument in the mouth region. From the mouth, the pharynx leads backwards to the oesophagus which occupies the fore part of the thorax. The inner walls of the oesophagus are folded. lengthways. The hinder part of the oesophagus is usually enlarged as a crop and its function is to store food. The last part of the fore intestine consists of a pear-shaped gizzard, sometimes called the proventriculus. Its walls are thick and muscular and there are many tooth-like projections from the inner wall for breaking up food. There is often a valve at the point of junction between the fore and mid-intestine which prevents food from passing forward from the mid to the fore intestine.

The mid-intestine: This is also called the mid-gut or stomach. It is sometimes bag-like, sometimes thin and looped or coiled. In the Cockroach there are a

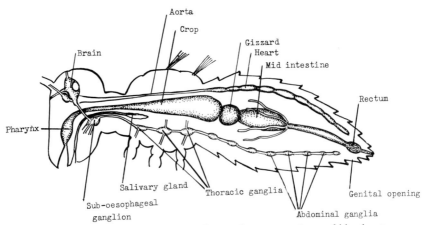

Fig. 1. Position of the alimentary canal, central nervous system and blood system in generalized (hypothetical) insect, from the side. Partly after Imms.

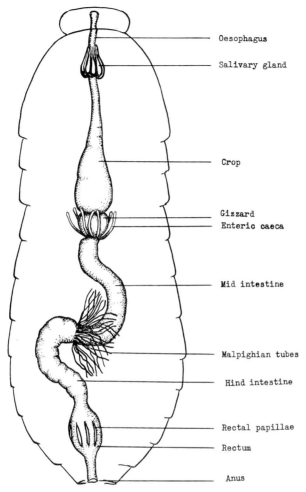

Fig. 2. Alimentary canal of the Cockroach. A partly diagram-
matic dissection, from above.

number of finger-like processes arising from the junction of the fore and
mid-intestine called enteric caeca, which increase the inner wall area. In
other insects they may be more numerous, fewer, or absent altogether. In
some larvae which feed on liquid matter, the mid-intestine is a closed sac
as when the nutrient material has been absorbed by the epithelial layer of
the mid-intestine, there is little or nothing left as a solid residue.

The hind intestine: It is usual for the hind intestine of most insects to show
three distinct regions as follows:

The small intestine, or ileum, the junction of which with the mid-intestine is normally shown by the presence of the pyloric valve and a number of thin hair-like tubes known as the Malpighian tubes (named after their discoverer, the Italian, Malpighi).

The large intestine or colon, from which in moths and beetles arises a hollow outgrowth or caecum.

The rectum is more or less globular or pear-shaped and bears on the inside a number of knob-like protrusions which have been called rectal glands. Their function is said to be the absorption of water from faecal matter. Water loss in an insect is a very important hazard and these rectal glands are one means of minimizing it. It is thought also that inorganic salts soluble in water may also be absorbed at this point.

The Nervous System

In all animals the nervous system is a connecting link between all the organs of sense, that is, all the organs which respond to the various sorts of stimuli such as light, touch, smell, taste, etc., and the muscles and glands. Nervous tissue is essentially composed of neurones or nerve-cells in a general supporting tissue. The nerve-cell usually bears a number of long filaments which enable it to maintain contact, either directly or in a series with other nerve-cells, between the sense organ and the 'effecting' organ, such as a muscle or a gland. Long conducting nerve-fibres are composed of a number of nerve-cells grouped together and such a fibre is called an axon. The nerve-cells are also grouped together as nervous centres or ganglia (singular, ganglion).

The nervous system of an insect is divided into three parts as follows:

1. *The central nervous system*

This is the most important part of the nervous system and is composed of a series of ganglia united in pairs sometimes so closely that they appear as one, and they are united by long nerve-fibre strands called connectives. The central nervous system of the Cockroach is shown in Fig. 3.

The brain. In a typical insect, there are a pair of ganglia in each segment of the body but often adjacent pairs may coalesce. This latter condition occurs in the head where the brain consists of three distinct but fused ganglia-masses. The largest part of the brain and also that part which innervates the eyes is the first part of the ganglia-masses. They are called the optic lobes and optic ganglia. It is of interest to note that those insects with large compound eyes have correspondingly large optic lobes and optic ganglia. The second part of the brain innervates the antennae and the swellings which are a feature of this part are known as the olfactory lobes.

The suboesophageal ganglion. The oesophagus or throat lies immediately under the brain and beneath this lies a double ganglion called the suboesophageal ganglion. Connectives join this ganglion to the brain by

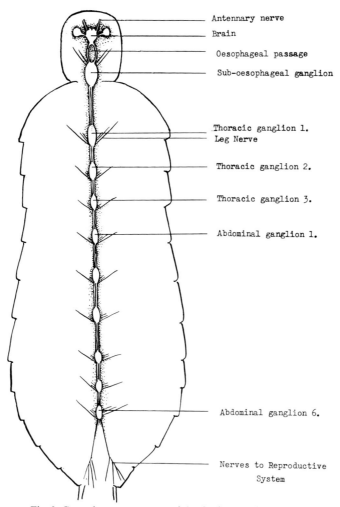

Antennary nerve

Brain

Oesophageal passage

Sub-oesophageal ganglion

Thoracic ganglion 1.
Leg Nerve

Thoracic ganglion 2.

Thoracic ganglion 3.

Abdominal ganglion 1.

Abdominal ganglion 6.

Nerves to Reproductive
System

Fig. 3. Central nervous system of the Cockroach, from above.

encircling the throat. This ganglion innervates the mouth-parts and the lower part of the head.

The ventral nerve-cord. The remainder of the central nervous system consists of a series of paired ganglia lying on the floor of the thorax and abdomen which constitutes the ventral nerve-cord. The first three pairs of ganglia are situated in the thorax and innervate the legs and the latter two pairs the wings also. The number of ganglia in the abdomen varies greatly in different insects. Often the first abdominal ganglia coalesce with the last thoracic ganglia.

2. *The visceral nervous system*

This is a series of three sympathetic nervous systems, the first of which innervates, principally, the intestine and heart. The second system innervates the spiracles, that is the outer openings of the tracheal system. The third system arises from the last ganglion of the abdominal nerve-cord. It innervates the reproductive system and the hinder part of the alimentary canal.

3. *The peripheral nervous system*

This system consists mainly of a delicate ramification of nerve-cells innervating many organs and sensory hairs and bristles arising from the integument and thus occurs just beneath the latter. In addition, part of this system is to be found on the wall of the alimentary canal. The peripheral nervous system arises from the central nervous system.

The Respiratory System of an Insect

In almost all insects, respiration, or gas exchange, takes place by means of a complex system of internal air-tubes which are known as tracheae. Air enters the body of the insect through small openings known as spiracles arranged in a series along both sides of the body. By means of the tracheae and the small tracheoles air is then conveyed directly to all parts of the body and the appendages. The aquatic larvae of some insects are furnished with gills, but this type of respiration is exceptional.

The function of the spiracle

This is to provide openings for air to enter the tracheal system, to restrict the entrance of deleterious substances and at the same time prevent water loss.

The number of spiracles

The number of spiracles present in insects varies greatly. In one type of arrangement there are two pairs present in the thorax and eight pairs present in the abdomen. Other types of spiracle arrangement appear to have been derived from this pattern by one or more pairs becoming nonfunctional. This is the general position in insect larvae. In the larvae of some species of two-winged flies there is a pair of spiracles present only in the prothorax and the last segment of the abdomen. In the larvae of some other species of two-winged flies, on the other hand, spiracles are present only on the last abdominal segment. This great reduction in the number of functional spiracles is said to be an adaption to life in water or a liquid medium.

The spiracle structure

Essentially, a spiracle consists of a horny margin leading to a vestibule which may be hairy or spiny to prevent the entrance of dust. It is provided with muscles which can close the spiracular entrance under certain conditions, such as when water loss may be excessive. Sometimes glands are present which, by secreting a water-repellent substance prevents the spiracle from getting wet, which would otherwise fill or clog with water and thus prevent the ingress of air.

The tracheae

When an insect is being dissected, the tracheal tubes may be identified by their silvery appearance due to the contained air. When highly magnified under the microscope the tracheal tube has a striated appearance. This has a spring-like action keeping the tracheae open and fully distended. The smallest tubes, the tracheoles, have a similar although much smaller structure. The diameter of the tracheoles is only about 1/125,000 of an inch!

The ends of the tracheoles may join up with other tracheoles to form a minute, delicate reticulated network over the surface of an organ or piece of tissue, or they may end inside the actual cells of muscle and other tissue.

In addition to the tracheae, many winged insects contain air-sacs which are special dilated thin-walled tracheae. The air-sacs act as a reservoir, increasing the amount of available air in the body of the insect, and, in addition, lower the specific gravity of the insect. This is, of course, a great advantage in flight.

Respiration

Oxygen travels through the tracheole walls inwards and carbon dioxide outwards by diffusion. The amount of carbon dioxide is less than the amount of oxygen used for respiration. It is also so much more permeable than oxygen that a substantial amount is lost through the general body surface of the insect and does not require to be specially expelled from the tracheal contents.

When the insect is walking or flying there is sufficient dilation and contraction of the tracheal system by muscular movement for the additional oxygen required to be drawn in through the spiracles.

The Reproductive System of an Insect

The reproduction system in insects shows a wide range of shape and structures but it is of interest to note that the embryonic appearance of both male and female systems is similar. The organs of reproduction are situated wholly in the abdomen and generally in the hinder part. The genital openings occur on the under-side of the abdomen. In the case of males, the penis is everted from a position normally behind the ninth abdominal segment, and in the case of females the genital opening lies on or behind the eighth or ninth segment.

Male reproductive system consists of the following organs:

1. *The testes* (singular is testis) are paired and consist of a number of testicular tubes or follicles. They may be situated either above, below or at the sides of the alimentary canal. The spermatozoa are produced by special zones of tissues in the testes and are released into the *vasa deferentia*.

2. *The vasa deferentia* (singular is vas deferens) are paired tubes leading from the testes to a reservoir (the vesicula seminalis) in which the spermatozoa are stored.

3. *The vesicula seminalis* may be a common receptacle or it may be paired (plural is vesiculae seminales).

4. *The single ejaculatory duct* leads from the vesiculae seminales to the external opening. It is strongly muscular and part of the organ may be everted to form the terminal aedeagus.

5. *The accessory glands* are special glands from one to three pairs in number associated with the male genital system. The secretions of these glands may mix with the spermatozoa or may, in appropriate cases, take part in the formation of spermatophores.

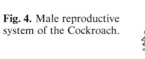
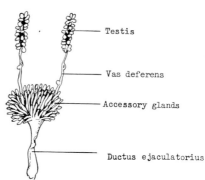

Fig. 4. Male reproductive system of the Cockroach.

Testis

Vas deferens

Accessory glands

Ductus ejaculatorius

Female reproductive system consists of the following organs:

1. *The ovaries.* There are two ovaries which lie on each side of the alimentary canal. Each ovary is made up of a number of tubes called ovarioles in which the eggs develop. At the apex of each ovariole is a terminal filament. All the filaments of each ovary join together before joining with the joined filaments of the ovary on the opposite side. At the apex of each ovariole is sited the tissue in which the germ-cells have their origin. As the germ-cells develop they pass down the ovariole tube towards the oviduct, being nourished by the special cells in the wall of the ovariole, and finally receive their skins and shells before being passed into the common oviduct.

2. *Common oviduct.* This is a muscular tube leading from the paired oviducts to the vagina.

3. *The vagina.* This consists of a shallow chamber arising from the hinder part of the eighth abdominal segment. In some insects there is a pouch-like extension known as the *bursa copulatrix*. It is of interest to note here that in the Common Furniture Beetle, *Anobium punctatum*, a pair of pouches arise from the vagina containing symbiotic yeasts which become attached to the eggs as they are laid. Thus, when the hatching larva emerges from the shell by consuming a part of it, the yeast-cells are transferred to its gut. The yeast-cells play an important part in the digestion of cellulose.

4. *The spermatheca* is also known as the *receptaculum seminis*. It arises as a pouch or duct from the vagina and serves to receive the spermatozoa and to store them until the developing eggs are in the condition for fertilization.

5. *The accessory glands.* These are known also as *colleterial glands*, of which there may be one or two pairs. They arise from the vagina and secrete substances associated with the eggs, such as the material for the egg-pod in Cockroaches and the cement enabling the eggs to adhere together in some other insects. The poison-glands of the wasps are special adaptions of the colleterial glands.

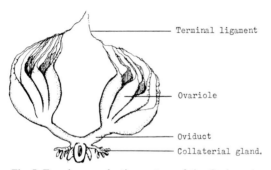

Fig. 5. Female reproductive system of the Cockroach.

Reproduction

Reproduction in insects is carried out by a typical sexual process whereby the male inserts the penis into the genital system of the female, via the vagina, and transfers spermatozoa. The latter are stored either by themselves or in a coherent body (a spermatophore) from which they escape. A spermatozoon fuses with an egg-cell to fertilize it and subsequently the egg is laid.

There are exceptions to this process. In some insects reproduction can take place without fertilization of the eggs by spermatozoa. This is known as *Parthenogenesis* and may occur periodically as a regular feature of the life-cycle or it may occur only occasionally and intermittently. In some insects more than one individual can develop from a single egg. This is called *Polyembryony*. A few insects are viviparous, most usually they produce living larvae direct from the vagina, the eggs having been retained within the oviduct or vagina to the hatching stage. Examples are known, however, in which prepupae, or adults, or nymphs are produced by the adult female.

The Skeletal System of Insects

The skeleton of an insect consists almost entirely of the integument enveloping its body. In many insects this integument or body wall is hard, being composed of a number of horny plates connected by an elastic membraneous skin to allow for movement. In other insects the integument is almost entirely membraneous although the head and jaws may be horny. The skeletal system, then, of an insect is entirely integumentary and being the outside layer it is known as the *Exoskeleton*.

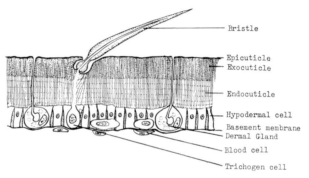

Fig. 6. Section of typical insect cuticle. Highly magnified. (After Wigglesworth.)

The Exoskeleton

The integument of an insect is built up of several layers, see Fig. 6 above. These are:

1. The outer layer or *Cuticle* which shows the following divisions: Commencing from the outside these are: the very thin epicuticle which is waxy and helps to prevent water loss; a much thicker exocuticle; and an even thicker laminated endocuticle. These three parts of the cuticle are non-living although complex processes may be elaborated within their structure.

2. The *Hypodermis*, which is a single layer of cells containing various glands associated with the cuticle, and specialized cells concerned with the moulting process (see later). It is the hypodermis which secretes the cuticle.

3. The *basement membrane* is a thin sheet of tissue adherent to the base of the hypodermis. It serves for the attachment of muscles and is also associated with blood-cells from which it is thought it might have its origin.

Chemical constitution of the cuticle. Reference has already been made to the horny cuticle of insects. It is usual to refer to the hardening of the cuticular

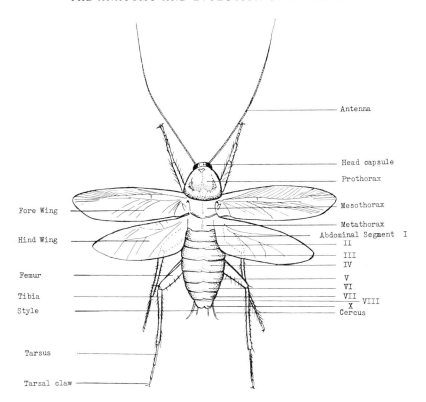

Fig. 7. The Cockroach with wings extended to show the main external features.

layer of insects as 'sclerotization'. It is of interest to note the chemical materials of which it is constituted. In the main two substances are associated together. These are chitin and protein and both contain nitrogen as well as carbon, hydrogen and oxygen. Chitin is a relatively stable substance being unaffected by water, alkalis, dilute acids and organic solvents.

The Shape of Insects

It has been estimated that there are about three and a half million different species of insects living in the world today and of these only about one-fifth have been described and named. In view of the wide range of adaption and form shown by insects, therefore, if an attempt is to be made to identify insect species, it is essential to understand the general pattern of insect shape and the essential parts of which the body is composed. We have already defined what an insect is by reference to its constituent parts and external and internal organs, so that we will now describe a whole insect, using the Cockroach as an example, see Fig. 7 above.

The head. The head is capsule-like and bears at its extremity the mouth parts. These consist of an upper lip, two pairs of jaws, (the mandibles and the maxillae) and the lower lip. The maxillae and the lower lip bear segmented tactile organs called palps. Illustrations of the mouth parts of certain insects are given later in the text in the descriptions of certain species of household insect pests.

The neck. The head is joined to the thorax by a small, for the most part, membraneous neck. The sclerotized areas are small, allowing for a certain amount of head movement both to and fro and forewards and backwards.

The thorax. The thorax is composed of three fairly distinct parts:

The *prothorax* bears the first pair of legs and the top surface is shield-shaped.

The *mesothorax* bears the second pair of legs and the first pair of wings (the fore wings).

The *metathorax* bears the third pair of legs and the second pair of wings (the hind wings).

The legs. The legs of insects consist of a number of articulating parts, and although in some insect species certain of these parts may be reduced or even missing, normally it is possible to refer the legs of insects to a common plan. Commencing from that part of the leg nearest to the body of the insect it is made up of the following parts:

The *coxa*, which is stout and of fair size.

The *trochanter*, which is usually small.

The *femur*, almost always long and stout.

The *tibia*, which is long and not quite so stout.

The *tarsus*, which consists of five small parts, the last terminating in a specially modified claw.

The wings. There are two pairs of wings in insects with the exception of:

(a) more primitive forms (an example being the silverfish, *Lepisma saccharina*).

(b) those groups of insects where one pair of wings are represented only by vestiges (an example being the order DIPTERA or two-winged flies).

(c) those insects that have evolved from winged groups but now do not possess wings, that is, they are secondarily wingless (an example being the FLEAS).

The wings of insects are modified in many ways and this is of importance in classification which is dealt with later. The wings of most insects possess veins which follow, to a greater or lesser extent, a common plan.

The abdomen. This consists of a number (usually not more than ten) of circular segments made up of a top horny part and a bottom horny part connected at the sides with membraneous cuticle. The last few segments are variously modified to form the genitalia. On account of the often highly complex nature of the genital apparatus, it is of great importance to the specialist in separating closely related species.

The Life-Cycle of an Insect

The period of time which elapses between the date when an egg is laid to the date when the individual produced from that egg lays further eggs (i.e. when it is sexually mature) is generally known as the life-cycle. It is, however, considered to be more correct to count this period starting from the date of fertilization of the insect to the date of death of the individual produced from that egg.

It can also mean, rather more loosely, the period between egg deposition and the emergence of the adult form, either from the pupal stage or the last immature stage. Strictly speaking, these are definitions of 'the length of the life-cycle' of an insect, the description of the life-cycle being a description of the various forms or stages which the insect undergoes before attaining sexual maturity.

There are, broadly speaking, two distinct types of insect life-cycle. In the

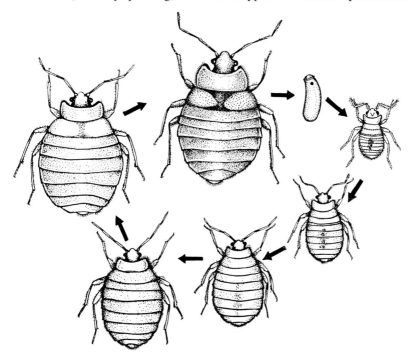

Fig. 8. Life-cycle of the Bed Bug (*Cimex lectularius*). This is an example of an insect exhibiting an incomplete metamorphosis, the various stages differing little from each other or from the adult. (Shown at the top centre.) Note that there is no pupal stage.

C

less highly developed group of insects of which the Bed Bug (*Cimex lectularius*) is given as an example (see Fig. 8), the individual produced from the egg is not unlike, in general appearance, the adult insect, and at each successive moult the shape of the insect more closely approximates to the appearance of the adult insect. This is well shown in the illustration. The Bed Bug, however, is an insect whose wings in the adult stage are very much reduced; two pads, representing the forewings only, are visible. These wing pads can be seen in the last of the immature stages.

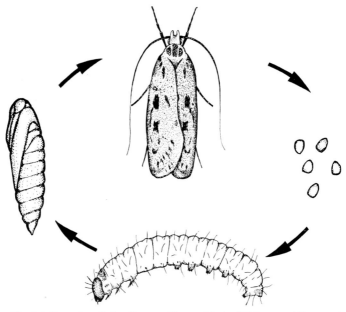

Fig. 9. Life-cycle of the Brown House Moth (*Hofmannophila pseudospretella*). This is an example of an insect exhibiting a complete metamorphosis, the various stages differing greatly from each other and from the adult. Here there is a pupal stage.

Insects which thus, during their life-cycle, pass through successive stages differing little from each other are said to exhibit an incomplete metamorphosis and are known as *Heterometabolous*. Insects which show the development of the wings on the outside of the body, that is, externally, are known as *Exopterygotous* insects. In the vast majority of cases, heterometabolous insects are exopterygotous, and vice versa.

In the more highly developed group of insects the different life-stages differ widely from each other and from the adult. The Brown House Moth (*Hofmannophila pseudospretella*) is given as an example of this type of life-cycle, see Fig. 9. From the egg, a larva (or grub or caterpillar) is hatched, which is the active stage and which does the eating and is mostly elongate in shape. Following the larval stage is the pupa (or chrysalis). The pupa is quiescent, does not eat, and can be looked upon as a resting stage. All the parts and organs of the adult insect are present in the pupa although not hardened or otherwise in a condition to carry out their various functions.

Insects which show this type of life-cycle, where there are abrupt changes in the shape and form of the immature life-stages, are said to exhibit a complete metamorphosis and are called *Holometabolous*. In the larval stage of these insects, the development of wings proceeds inside the body, such a circumstance being called *Endopterygotous*, Thus, holometabolous insects are endopterygotous and vice versa.

In insects, there is a wide range of shape in the larvae of holometabolous insects and many different forms will be described in the following pages. Two fairly distinct groups can usually be differentiated (see Fig. 10), the *Campodeiform* type (A) and the *Scarabaeiform* type (B).

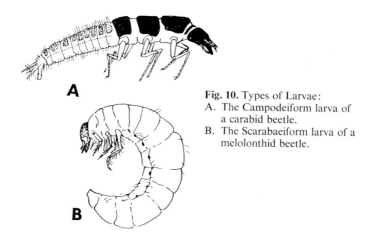

A

B

Fig. 10. Types of Larvae:
A. The Campodeiform larva of a carabid beetle.
B. The Scarabaeiform larva of a melolonthid beetle.

The Campodeiform larva is agile, often predaceous and usually sclerotised. The Scarabaeiform type can only move slowly, is not usually predaceous and is often whitish with a thin membraneous skin.

How Insects Grow

Growth in insects is confined to the immature stages. In those insects with a complete metamorphosis, this is confined to the larval stage, growth not taking place during the pupal stage. In those insects where the metamorphosis is incomplete, growth occurs during all the immature stages with the exception of the egg. In neither group of insects does growth occur during the adult stage, although it is a popular misconception that this is so.

It will be appreciated that growth in insects cannot take place in the same manner as in vertebrate animals (those with an internal skeleton and a backbone), the hard rigid external skeleton precluding this. Growth in insects, therefore, must take place by a periodic casting of the external skeleton, the growth-resisting skin. At each moulting, or *ecdysis*, as it is known, the immature insect is provided with a larger, although at first more loosely fitting, external covering. At the ecdysis the whole of the cuticle is renewed, even the lining of the fore and hind intestine and most of the tracheal system, and a new cuticle is developed by the under-lying hypodermal cells. In some household insects the old cast skins (which are sometimes called *exuviae*) are a feature of an infestation such as in the case of the Bed Bug and the Fur Beetle. The new cuticle of an insect immediately after ecdysis is creamy white and soft but rapidly hardens on contact with air. The different stages of a larval insect between ecdysis is known as an instar and when a larva hatches from the egg it is said to be in its first instar.

How Insects Evolved and how they are Classified

The first insects known from fossil records occurred in the Devonian period and were wingless, rather like the modern Springtails (*Collembola*) which are found under damp wood and stones, and, indeed, are occasionally found in damp kitchens (see Fig. 13). When something is moved from under the kitchen sink they are seen to jump away and the housewife may think they are something more harmful. It is of interest to note that the insect is able to jump by the springing of the forwardly directed organs which arise from the hinder part of the abdomen. The wingless groups are the more primitive insects and an example well known to almost everyone is the Bristletail, known as the Silverfish, in the group THYSANURA.

These primitive wingless groups (such a group is known as an order) are placed together into a subclass known as the APTERYGOTA.

The winged insects which constitute the other subclass, the PTERYGOTA, are first known as fossils from the lower part of the Upper Carboniferous strata. The orders consituting the older group are found to be those showing the external development of wings and the metamorphosis is slight, there being no pupal stage. This division is   known as the EXOPTERYGOTA (named after the external wing growth) but another name often given to this division is based on the metamorphosis. This is the HEMIMETABOLA.

The more modern insects are placed in the division ENDOPTERYGOTA, in which internal development of wings takes place and a complete metamorphosis is shown, including a pupal stage. Fossil forms of these insects are first found in the Lower Permian.

The Insect Orders

The natural orders in which insects are placed usually give little difficulty to the students of insect life as most would be able to recognise a beetle (COLEOPTERA), a two-winged fly (DIPTERA), a butterfly or moth (LEPIDOPTERA) and some of the other more important insect orders.

A Synopsis of the more important Insect Orders with special attention given to those orders containing Household Insect Pests

APERYGOTA

Order 1. Bristletails (THYSANURA). Mouth parts for biting. Body clothed with scales. Abdomen terminating in cerci and a median filament. The Silverfish belongs to this group.

Order 4. Springtails (COLLEMBOLA). Mouth parts for biting. Abdomen with leaping appendage.

PTERYGOTA

EXOPTERYGOTA

Order 9. Grasshoppers, Locusts and Crickets (ORTHOPTERA). Forewings leathery. Mouth parts for biting. Female generally with well-developed ovipositor.

Order 11. Earwigs (DERMAPTERA). Mouth parts for biting. Forewings small and leathery, hindwings large and membraneous, folded beneath forewings when at rest. Abdomen terminates in forceps.

Order 13. The Cockroaches and Mantids (DICTYOPTERA). Legs for running, cerci segmented, forewings leathery, ovipositor concealed. Eggs are laid in pouch-like cases. Long filamentous antennae.

Order 14. Termites (ISOPTERA). Mouth parts for biting. Both pairs of wings similar or they may be absent. In wingless forms eyes are also absent. Social insects living in communities of greater or lesser complexity. No British species but of great economic importance in tropical and subtropical countries.

Order 16. Book Lice or Psocids (PSOCOPTERA). Mouth parts for biting. Wings membraneous with reduction in veins. Very small insects. Antennae long, many jointed.

Order 17. Biting Lice (MALLOPHAGA). Mouth parts for biting. Most species found on birds were they feed on pieces of skin and feathers. Wings absent. Eyes reduced.

Order 18. Sucking Lice (ANOPLURA). Mouth parts for piercing and sucking. Found only on mammals on which they feed by puncturing the skin and sucking blood. Wings absent. Eyes reduced. The body and head louse are in this order.

Order 19. Plant Bugs, Frog Hoppers, Aphids, Scale Insects, Water Scorpions, Water Boatmen (HEMIPTERA). Mouth parts for piercing and sucking. Wings with few veins and either forewings leathery or basal half-leathery. Includes the Bed Bug.

Order 20. Thrips (THYSANOPTERA). Small insects with specialized mouth parts to break the tissues of plants and suck the sap. Wings long and narrow, fringed with long hairs. Often enter houses fortuitously and can sometimes be seen in framed pictures where their small size has enabled them to enter cracks.

ENDOPTERYGOTA

Order 21. The Lacewings (NEUROPTERA). Mouth parts for sucking in larvae, biting in adults. Wings membraneous with many cross-veins. Predaceous larvae.

Order 23. Butterflies and Moths (LEPIDOPTERA). Larval mouth parts for biting, In adults mouth parts modified into a long coiled tube, and mandibles absent. Wings covered with scales often brightly coloured.

Order 25. Two-winged Flies (DIPTERA). Highly modified mouth parts for biting in larvae and sucking or piercing and sucking in adults. Forewings membraneous, hindwings minute, modified as balancing organs. Larvae are legless.

Order 26. The Fleas (SIPHONAPTERA or APHANIPTERA). Small insects, wingless and laterally compressed. Eyes always simple if present. Antennae short and stout, reposing in grooves. Mouth parts for piercing and sucking. Larvae are legless. Adults are parasitic on warm-blooded animals.

Order 27. Ants, Bees, Wasps, Sawflies, Ichneumon Flies, etc. (HYMENOPTERA). Mouth parts for biting or sucking in adults and for biting in most larvae. Two pairs of membraneous wings, forewings larger and linked by a row of hooks to fore-edge of hindwing. First abdominal segment fused with thorax. Ovipositor often modified for sawing, piercing or stinging.

Order 28. Beetles (COLEOPTERA). Mouth parts for biting in larvae and adults, for biting and sucking in some larvae. Forewings modified as hard leathery covers (Elytra) for membraneous functional hindwings. Wings have few veins. The largest order in the animal kingdom, of which there are a quarter of a million described species. About 3700 species are found in the British Isles.

How Insects are Classified

The broad divisions into which the class INSECTA is divided have now been described down as far as the insect Order and the main characteristics of the principal insect orders have been given. We shall now see how the orders of insects are subdivided.

The insect Order is divided into a number of primary divisions called suborders, which in turn are divided into groups called families. It is usual for the name of an insect family to end in -IDAE, for example the name of the family of the LEPIDOPTERA to which the Common Clothes Moth *Tineola bisselliella* belongs, is the TINAEIDAE. In many cases, but not all, the families are divided into subfamilies, in which case it is usual for the name to end in -INAE. In all cases, however, the families or subfamilies are divided into the smallest groups known as Genera (singular is Genus). Each genus is made up of one or more distinct kinds known as species.

It must be emphasized that the classification of insects is a natural one, insects being classified in the way that they have evolved, closely related species being placed together. The closest relationship is thus the genus, then the subfamily and then the family.

How Insects are Named

It will have been observed that the scientific name of an insect consists of two words. The first word of the name is the name of the genus, that is, the smallest group of related species, and it is spelt with a capital letter. The second word of the name is the name of the species and it is always spelt with a small letter. In manuscript and typescript both words are underlined to signify that they would appear in italics when printed. The name given to a genus is never duplicated although this may be so in the case of specific names. Thus the combination of the generic name and the individual specific name can only mean one particular species and, furthermore, its relationship with a group of species can be seen at once. More correctly, the name of the author who first described and named the insect according to the Linnaean system described above should follow the name either in full or in abbreviated form, but this rule need not be adopted on every occasion.

This Linnaean system of naming animals (named after its founder Linnaeus 1707–78) has been universally adopted and it has enabled the naming of insects to be conducted in an exact manner. That is not to say that complications and anomalies never arise, but, taken generally, the system works very well.

Part II

3

SILVERFISH AND SPRINGTAILS

Thysanura and *Collembola*

With this chapter commences a detailed description of all the common household insect pests listed previously. They are dealt with in the order of the natural classification.

APTERYGOTA

THYSANURA (Bristletails)

The Silverfish, *Lepisma saccharina.* (See Plate I)

This primitive wingless insect is so called on account of its shining grey coloration, its sinuous movements and perhaps its quick darts to cover when it is disturbed. The Silverfish is nocturnal, shuns the light and is perhaps most often seen when uncovered in dampish situations such as in kitchens and sculleries. Although it is able to walk up rough vertical surfaces such as wallpaper and plaster, it is unable to walk up vertical smooth surfaces of porcelain and glass, so that in this way it is often found trapped in baths and basins.

Appearance. This is readily seen from the Plate. The absence of wings, shining grey colour, long antennae, torpedo shape and the three long bristles at the end of the abdomen serve to render identification an easy matter. In addition to the long bristles there are several pairs of short appendages called 'styles' on the under-side of the last abdominal segment. It is about half an inch in length. In Fig. 11 is shown the two pairs of toothed mouth parts, the mandibles and the maxillae which are used for scraping fungus-softened wallpaper before eating. The compound eyes, each consisting of twelve separate eyes, are also shown.

Economic importance. The Silverfish is responsible for little actual damage. It feeds on carbohydrate substances such as starch used for wallpaper paste, and damp wallpaper (where it is probably able to digest the cellulose). It is also recorded as biting small irregular shaped holes in linen, cotton and artificial silk. Its carbohydrate diet is probably supplemented by protein from dead insects and sizes and glues used in book-binding. It must also be remembered that in the damp situations which it inhabits fungal moulds are present which may not only be browsed by the insect but certainly soften and break down paper and such materials as book-bindings. The Silverfish cannot be looked upon as being of economic importance but

43

it is an unpleasant inhabitant of our homes and gives rise to feelings of revulsion.

Life-cycle

Egg. About a hundred eggs are laid by each female, singly or in batches of two or three in crevices and under objects. They are oval in shape 1·5 × 1·0 mm. in size and are at first white and smooth but they soon become brownish and wrinkled.

Nymphal stages. During the first three months the insect is whitish, being devoid of the silvery, spade-shaped scales that make their appearance at the third moult. The external genital appendages appear at the eighth moult, but it is not known at what stages the insect becomes fully mature and there may be some variations amongst the individuals according to environment. An interesting feature, however, of the Silverfish is that it goes on moulting throughout its life and in doing so is able to regenerate organs such as legs which have been accidentally lost.

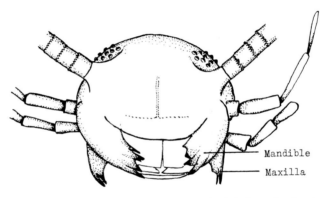

Fig. 11. Head of Silverfish (*Lepisma saccharina*) from the front, showing the two pairs of jaw-like mouth parts.

Length of life-cycle. Incubation of the eggs last from 19 days at 32°C. to 43 days at 22°C. and it has been recorded that the nymphal stage takes from 90 to 120 days at 27°C. The adult is very long-lived, living 3½ years at 27°C., 2 years at 29°C. and 1½ years at 32°C. It is stated that the eggs of Silverfish do not hatch above 50 per cent relative humidity at 22°C. and that the optimum relative humidity for maturation is 90 per cent.

The Firebrat, *Thermobia domestica.* (See Fig. 12)

Appearance. In general the Firebrat is somewhat like the Silverfish; it is, however, rather larger and wider and has not the metallic appearance, being greyish-white with darker speckled markings.

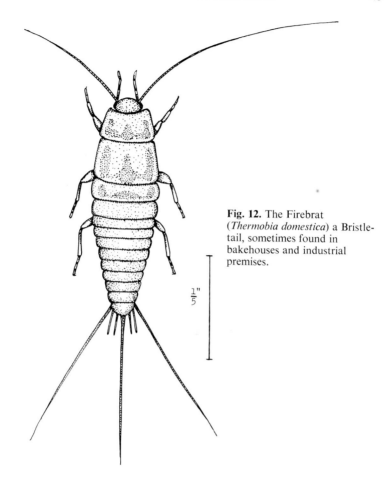

Fig. 12. The Firebrat (*Thermobia domestica*) a Bristletail, sometimes found in bakehouses and industrial premises.

$\frac{1}{5}$"

Economic importance. Although both insects are found only indoors, they inhabit very different situations. Whereas the Silverfish requires very humid conditions, the Firebrat is found only where it is very warm, or even hot, such as in bakeries, restaurant kitchens or in factories where much steam is used, but a high humidity is not a necessity. Similar food is taken to that of the Silverfish, but it may take a higher proportion as crumbs or other waste food.

Life-cycle

Egg. These are a little smaller than those of silverfish being 1·0 × 0·8 mm.

Nymphal stages. There is an indeterminate number of moults which may be up to 60. Scales are acquired only at the fourth stage.

Length of life-cycle. Incubation of the eggs takes from 77 days at 25°C. to 9 days at 44°C., and maturation takes from 330 days at 27°C. to 47 days at 42°C. The adult life is from 2 to 2½ years at 32°C. and from 1 to 1½ years at 37°C.

COLLEMBOLA (Springtails). (See Fig. 13)

These small primitive wingless insects never exceed a quarter of an inch in length. They are very numerous in nature and act as scavengers in the soil, amongst dead leaves and other vegetable detritus. As indoor pests they are never serious, but some species are nevertheless often found in kitchens, outhouses, cellars or verandahs in damp, dark situations. When disturbed they may jump several inches into the air, probably in an effort to evade

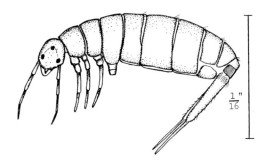

Fig. 13. A Springtail (COLLEMBOLA). Note the paired leaping organ at the hinder end of the abdomen.

the attentions of predatory animals. They are certainly very successful in becoming invisible very quickly after two or three jumps. If a bucket or a tree pot is moved suddenly, Springtails are often seen jumping themselves into a new position. Jumping is brought about by a stout, forked tail which bends under the abdomen and is there held in position until released by a small organ on the third abdominal segment. When it springs backwards the tail propels the light, fragile insect into the air.

The anatomy of Springtails is remarkable in that the antennae are composed of only four segments and there are only six segments in the abdomen, which is the smallest number found in any insect.

Collembola do not undergo a larval and pupal stage, the young Springtails being similar to the parent in shape when they hatch from the egg. Springtails require a very high atmospheric humidity and shun light. The different species show preference for different foodstuffs but most seem to subsist on vegetable and animal debris and occasionally on living plants, but very little economic damage is caused.

4

THE COCKROACHES, CRICKET AND EARWIG

Dictyoptera, Orthoptera and *Dermaptera*

We now consider household insect pests belonging to the immensely larger group, the winged insects or PTERYGOTA, and we commence with those insects considered to be at the lowest stage of evolutionary development and proceed to those at the higher stage.

EXOPTERYGOTA
DICTYOPTERA

The Common Cockroach, Oriental Cockroach or 'Black Beetle', *Blatta orientalis.*

Appearance. The adult insects are shiny chocolate brown in colour and about one inch in length. The males possess wings which cover the abdomen to the extent of about two-thirds, but the wings of the female are reduced to short lobes which reach only as far as the hind margin of the thorax. The first segment of the thorax, the prothorax, is large and shield-shaped and the antennae are long and whip-like.

Life-cycle. (Shown in Fig. 14)

Egg. The female lays approximately 16 eggs at a time in a large, horny, dark brown egg-case or capsule which is about half an inch in length and about a quarter of an inch broad. The female carries the egg-case about, partly extruded, before she deposits it in a warm sheltered situation, usually near a food supply. She is able to lay a maximum of 9 capsules.

Nymphal stages. The nymphs escape when the egg-capsule splits along the dorsal ridge and it is usual for only 10 to 15 to hatch from one capsule. The young nymphs moult immediately, appearing pale yellow at first but after a few hours they darken to dark brown. The nymphs moult 6 to 10 times, each time increasing in size until the final moult to the adult stage (see Fig. 17).

Adult stage. Pairing takes place soon after the final moult but the first egg-capsule is not ready for deposition until 10 to 14 days after this.

Length of life-cycle. The total length depends very much on the suitability and abundance of food as well as temperature and humidity, and in addi-

47

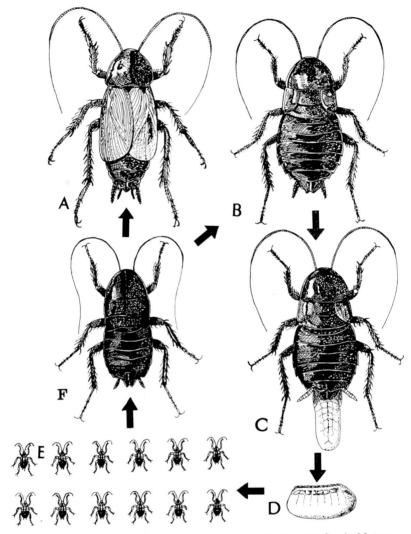

Fig. 14. The life-cycle of the Common Cockroach, *Blatta orientalis:* A. Mature male; B. Mature female; C. Female bearing egg-case; D. Egg-case; E. Young nymphs; F. Last stage nymph.

tion there appears to be wide variation amongst individuals. The eggs of this species hatch in 81 days at 21°C., 57 days at 25°C. and 42 days at 30°C. The nymphal stages take 530 days at 25°C and 300 days at 30°C. At 25°C. the adults were found to live 140 days.

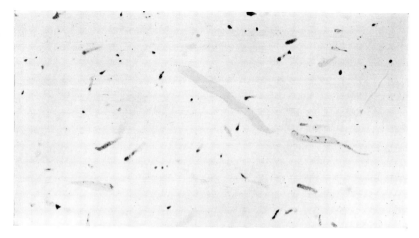

Fig. 15. Stains of the Common Cockroach on paper.

Fig. 16. Bread damaged and stained by the Common Cockroach.

D

Economic importance. In the United Kingdom this is the most common species of Cockroach in bakeries, restaurants, hotels and houses. They attack a wide range of food products fouling what they do not consume (see Figs. 15 and 16). A disgusting odour is associated with these insects, known as the 'roachy' smell, which is a sure sign of contamination. Cockroaches appear to show some degree of gregariousness as they are often seen to cluster together in suitable conditions. The Common Cockroach is perhaps more gregarious than the other species.

Fig. 17. Cockroach moulting. Note hanging
position.

The German Cockroach, Steamfly or Shiner, *Blattella germanica.* (See Plate I and Fig. 18)

Appearance. The adult insects are from 12 to 14 mm. (about ⅝ in.) in length and are yellowish-brown in colour with two dark brown longitudinal bands on the prothorax. The female is slightly larger and fatter than the male, but both sexes possess fully developed wings which are sometimes put to use when the insects are disturbed. This species is very active and it is a more rapid and prolific breeder than the Oriental Cockroach.

Life-cycle

Egg. The eggs are laid in characteristic egg-cases which are carried about by the female, partially extruded at the end of the abdomen, for from two

Fig. 18. German Cockroach with egg-case.

to four weeks. The glossy brown egg-case is roughly rectangular, contains from 20 to 40 eggs and is $\frac{1}{4}$ in. in length and $\frac{1}{8}$ in. broad.

Nymphal stages. The egg-case (see Fig. 19) is dropped as soon as the young nymphs are ready to hatch and it splits along the ridge. They struggle free head foremost and immediately moult. There are six moults altogether.

Adult stage. Pairing takes place from a week to a fortnight after the final moult and oviposition begins 4 to 7 days later. One mating will fertilize all the eggs and the female is capable of laying up to 7 capsules. The formation of the succeeding capsules commences about a week after the preceding one has been laid.

Length of life-cycle. It has been observed that at 25°C. the adults lived

Fig. 19. Egg-case of German Cockroach. Enlarged.

260 days. The eggs hatch in 24 days at 21°C., 28 days at 25°C. and 15 days at 30°C., and the nymphal stages are passed through in 172 days at 21°C., 103 days at 25°C. and 74 days at 30°C. The adults of this species are unable to live long without food, dying from starvation in from 2 to 6 weeks at 25°C. The nymphs die in 3 weeks if kept without food.

Economic importance. This insect is the smallest of the domestic species of Cockroach and often infests large premises, especially those which are centrally heated and where the air is moist and the temperature is around 70°F. A wide variety of stored foods are attacked and damage by nymphal stages and adults to boots, hair and skins is reported. In domestic premises these insects are often found in kitchens often in the vicinity of the stove and sink. This insect is cosmopolitan, and is found in most parts of the world where it is sufficiently warm. It appears to be more dependent on moisture than *Blatta orientalis*. The German Cockroach is not usually found out of doors in Britain. Distribution is commonly effected by transportation in wooden cases, cartons and packing material of various sorts.

ORTHOPTERA

The House Cricket *Gryllulus domesticus.* (See Plate I)

The House Cricket is related to the grasshoppers and locusts. It can, however, be differentiated from species in these groups by the way in which the wings are carried. They lie flat on the back with the sides folded around the body. The grasshoppers and locusts, on the other hand, carry the wings tent-like along the body. The House Cricket is perhaps best known on account of the shrill chirping noise that it makes by rubbing the serrated edges of the fore wings against each other. Only the males produce

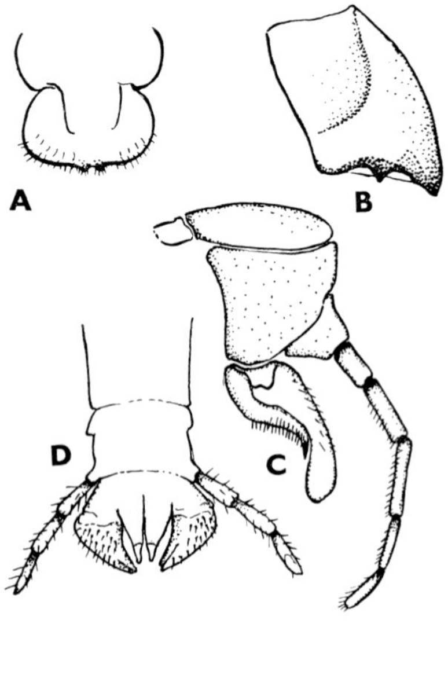

Fig. 20. Mouth parts of a Cricket dissected:
A. Labrum (upper lip)
B. Mandible, one of pair
C. Maxilla with palp, one of pair
D. Labium with palps (Lower lip)

the noise and it is perceived by the females through auditory organs located on the front pair of legs. Formerly the noise made by the Cricket was thought to be a welcome homely sound but today it 'gets on the nerves' and produces extreme annoyance.

Appearance. This is readily seen from Plate I. The antennae are long and thin and the body is pale fawn to greyish-yellow in colour mottled with brown. The femora of the hind legs are large and strong. The mouth parts are primitive in type, adapted for biting (see Fig. 20). At the hinder end of the abdomen there is a pair of long, slightly curved cerci and the female possesses a long ovipositor. In size they vary from a half to three-quarters of an inch in length.

Life cycle

Egg. The whitish-yellow banana-shaped eggs are 2·5 mm. in length and 0·5 mm. wide and are laid in cracks and crevices in buildings or in soft soil on rubbish dumps. From 40 to 170 or even more eggs are laid by one female and are said to be very sensitive to atmospheric conditions, shrivelling in dry conditions or attacked by fungi when damp. The eggs hatch in from 1 to 10 weeks mainly dependent on temperature.

Nymphal Stages. The first-stage nymphs are grey in colour and about one-tenth of an inch in length and the time taken for all the seven nymphal stages to take place varies from 50 days to 33 weeks according to temperature. Indeed, this insect is very dependent on warmth and it is only in warm situations where it is found, such as bakeries, industrial premises, kitchens and near boilers. Out of doors it is often found in rubbish-dumps where fermenting and decaying vegetable refuse provides the necessary warmth. Neither the nymphs nor the adults are active in cold conditions and they are not able to survive much more than a week's starvation.

Economic importance. The Cricket is not a native British insect but originates in the hot deserts stretching from the Sahara to Persia. It is not able to survive out of doors during the British winter except in special circumstances so that those insects living on rubbish dumps must seek shelter in warm buildings in the autumn or succumb. Mostly the Cricket is a scavenger but foodstuffs left lying about at night will be eaten. Soft foods are preferred such as vegetables, cooked or raw, meat cooked or raw, bread, dough and other soft substances used in the confectionery trade. The Cricket has the peculiar habit of nibbling materials on which it is not feeding and sometimes causes extensive damage to textiles of wool, cotton, and artificial silk, and is recorded also as damaging leather and wood. In assessing the economic importance of this insect, due notice must be taken of the great annoyance which is caused by the chirruping.

DERMAPTERA

The Earwig *Forficula auricularia.* (See Fig. 21)

The common European Earwig is one of nine native British insects in this order. The order DERMAPTERA contains only about 900 world species. The word 'earwig' is of historical significance on account of the widespread belief that they are liable to make their way into the human ear. Reports of this actually taking place are known to the writer.

Fig. 21. *Forficula auricularia*: the Common Earwig, with wings extended.

Appearance. The earwig is almost too well known to require description but nevertheless a few brief notes are given here. The body length varies from 10 to 14 mm., the forceps adding another 4 to 9 mm. The colour is a dark sienna brown but the head is a little darker and the legs are a little paler. The first pair of wings are scale-like and serve to cover the folded hind pair of membraneous wings, but the insect seldom flies. Most persons, however, would identify the Earwig by its possession of the cerci or forceps at the end of the abdomen. These are curved in the male but straight in the females. The function of the forceps is unknown, the most probable suggestion being that they are used as a warning to predatory animals.

Life cycle

Egg. In spring, the female lays a batch of about 30 eggs in cells beneath the soil surface. The white oval eggs are about $1 \cdot 0 \times 1 \cdot 25$ mm. in size and they are looked after by the mother.

Nymphal stages. After hatching the mother looks after the young nymphs for a few days before they disperse. Four nymphal stages usually occur although it is recorded that six have occurred from time to time. Except for being wingless the nymphs resemble the adults.

Length of life-cycle. There seems to be little information on this subject but it is virtually certain that the Common Earwig undergoes one life-cycle annually and hibernates in the adult stage.

Economic importance. The Common Earwig can only be termed an intruder into the household, a wanderer from the garden. It is nocturnal in habit and hides during the daylight hours in crevices, and it is probably in search of the latter that it makes its way under doors and through badly fitted windows. In the garden they do a little damage by gnawing holes on flower petals but on the other hand they do a certain amount of good by destroying other insects. From time to time, however, they occur in very large numbers in houses, which is probably due to an acute scarcity of suitable crevice-like hiding places out of doors.

5

LICE

Book Louse, Head and Body Lice and Dog Lice

Psocoptera, Mallophaga and Anoplura

This chapter deals with those insects commonly called Lice. Such insects belong to several orders of insects and the word usually connotes a parasitic habit. Aphids (green fly and black fly) are sometimes called Plant Lice because they are directly parasitic on plants. The first insect which we describe, however, the Book Louse, is not a parasite.

It is of interest to note that Fish Lice and Wood Lice are not insects but belong to the class CRUSTACEA.

PSOCOPTERA (Book Lice), sometimes called 'Psocids'.

Liposcelis divinatorius

Appearance. Several species of Book Lice are found indoors. They are of rather similar appearance but the species cited has been more widely investigated. They are very small insects with soft bodies, creamish to greyish or light brown in colour. Wings are usually absent from those species commonly found indoors although other species possess two pairs. A pair of wing-pads may be present. In many species, including that cited, males are absent, parthenogenetic reproduction being the rule. The head is relatively large as are the antennae, but the eyes are poorly developed. The femora are enlarged as though it were able to leap but such is not the case. The insect, however, can run quickly and it is this habit which causes the householder to be aware of its presence. One interesting habit shown by the species *Trogium pulsatorium* is the tapping noise which it produces by vibrating its abdomen against a material such as paper. It is probable that the first reference to the 'Death Watch' concerned this Book Louse and not the wood-boring beetle.

Life-cycle

Egg. The 'bluish-pearly' eggs are relatively very large, being about one-third of the size of the adult insect. They are laid singly and are sticky so that they become cemented to the material on which they are laid.

Nymphal stages. In the cited species there are 4 nymphal stages which are similar in most respects to the adult but are paler in colour. In other species, however, the number of observed nymphal stages varies from three to eight.

Length of life-cycle. The following information concerns the species *Liposcelis divinatorius.* The eggs hatch in 11 days at 25°C. and 75 per cent relative humidity. At first three eggs are laid daily but later this drops to one per week. The nymphal stage lasts only 15 days and when fed in the laboratory on a diet of high nutritional value, such as yeast, the adult lives for six months. The total number of eggs laid is 200. This species dies if exposed to 0°C. for 3 hours but requires a 24-hour exposure to 42·5°C. and 75 per cent relative humidity to produce death. It cannot develop at relative humidities less than 55 per cent at 25°C. or 65 per cent at 35°C.

Economic importance. Pscoids live on fungi growing on the surface of such materials as books, woodwork, paper, plaster and leather. Books are especially susceptible to mould growth due to the glues and sizes used, but it must be emphasized that in all cases the psocids are feeding on the moulds produced by humid conditions. For this reason they are common in newly built houses during the time the plaster is drying out and there is general dampness. Psocids will also infest decaying farinaceous foodstuffs left about for pets. They are absent from dry well-ventilated buildings.

Those insects more usually known as 'lice' belong to two main groups, the members of which, although similar in that they are external parasites of other animals, differ considerably in external shape and in the method of obtaining food from the host.

These groups are:

1. The MALLOPHAGA, known as Biting Lice or Bird Lice. Although a few species are found on mammals (certain species infest domestic animals) they are predominantly pests of birds. The first segment of the body—the pronotum—is distinct and free and the mouth parts are adapted for biting. For the most part food is obtained from feather, fur and skin fragments although some species are known to suck blood from wounds. There are about 2600 different species in the world.

2. The ANOPLURA sometimes called the SIPHUNCULATA.

These are known as Sucking Lice. All are parasitic on mammals. The thoracic segments are fused together, the pronotum not being distinct as in the MALLOPHAGA, and the mouth parts are adapted for piercing skin and sucking blood. All ANOPLURA do this exclusively. There are about 225 known species throughout the world.

In neither group is there the slightest vestige of wings, and the two groups are also similar in that there is no metamorphosis in the life cycle—the young nymphal stages being, in most respects, except that of size and maturation of reproduction organs, similar to the adults.

MALLOPHAGA (Biting Lice)

Dog Biting Louse, *Trichodectes canis.* (See Fig. 22.) This is the most usual biting louse found indoors and of the two species of louse found on dogs is by far the commonest.

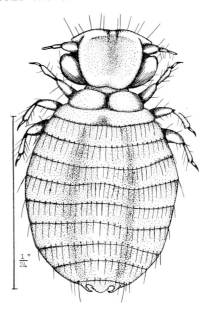

Fig. 22. The Dog Biting Louse, *Trichodectes canis*.

Appearance. It is about 1/16 in. in length and brownish in colour. It is flattened from top to bottom which serves as a good distinguishing feature from the flea, which is flattened from side to side. The shape of the insect is shown in the figure and the characteristic flatness of the head should be noted. This can be seen with the naked eye by a sharp-sighted person who can thus distinguish this species from the Dog Sucking Louse (*Linognathus setosus*). The latter insect has a rather smaller head, is greyish in colour and the abdomen is rather longer and more pointed.

Life-cycle. The eggs are cemented to the base of an individual hair and the nymphal stages are very similar to the adult in shape. The entire life-cycle takes place on the dog's body.

Economic importance. The Dog Biting Louse is parasitic throughout its life and subsists on bits of dead skin. They are more commonly found on certain areas of the dog's body; from the ears down to the base of the neck is the more usual situation followed by the saddle and flanks and the base of the tail. Lice are transferred by bodily contact and their presence can be diagnosed if the dog should suddenly and nervously try to reach high up on its flank with its nose, or, standing on three legs, endeavour to reach the same part with its hind paws. In addition, an infested dog will sit quickly and then urgently try to sink its nose in the base of the tail or try to allay an irritation at the back of the ear with a hind paw.

Other biting lice may be accidentally brought into the kitchen as they are often very common parasites of poultry. The dust baths often taken by fowls and other birds are an endeavour to rid themselves of the attentions of these parasites. Biting Lice, however, soon fall off a dead bird, or, adhering to the feathers, are otherwise disposed of.

ANOPLURA (Sucking Lice)

All the members of this group are parasitic on mammals and without exception suck the blood of their hosts, their mouth parts being specially modified for piercing the skin and sucking. The members of the family PEDICULIDAE are parasitic on man and monkeys, and are the only suck-ing lice to possess eyes. There are two species of lice attacking man, the Human Louse, *Pediculus humanus*, and the Crab Louse or Pubic Louse, *Phthirus pubis*. The former species, which is by far the most important, exists in two forms or varieties. These are the Head Louse, known as var. *capitis*, and the Body Louse, known as var. *corporis*.

The two species may be distinguished from each other by *Pediculus* possessing legs which are all approximately equally strong, although the first pair of legs of the male are rather stouter than those of the female. In *Phthirus*, on the other hand, the first legs are slender, terminating in a long fine claw, but the second and third legs are strong with thick claws. In addition, in *Pediculus* the abdomen is about twice as long as broad whilst in *Phthirus* it is broader than it is long.

The Head Louse, *Pediculus humanus* var *capitis.*

Appearance. The form of this insect is shown in the figure. In colour they vary from a dirty white to greyish black, the coloration being more pro-nounced on the more highly sclerotized parts of the body. The degree of coloration of the adult is dependent on the hair coloration of its host during the nymphal stages only. Thus, if the nymphal stages are passed on a person of blonde coloration the adult louse is light in colour, but if they are passed on a person of dark hair colouring then the resulting adult is more pronounced in coloration.

Life-cycle.

Egg. Eggs are laid by the female close to the base of the hair near the scalp and as the egg is laid a quantity of adhesive cement covers its base so that the egg is firmly cemented to the hair. This cement is so hard that long after the young nymph has left the egg, the empty shell remains fixed to the hair and grows out with the hair. The eggs (and the empty shell) are known as 'nits' and are nearly oval. They are pearly white in colour and 0·8 mm. in length and 0·3 mm. wide. The hatched egg is easily identified by its opalescent and translucent appearance. Just before hatching the eyes and other structure of the embryo can be made out through the trans-lucent shell. On hatching, the top of the egg falls off like a lid.

Nymphal stages. There are three nymphal stages, all of which resemble the adult except in size and possession of sexual organs, but there is some change in colour. During the first stage the nymph is a pale straw colour.

The gut of the nymph is visible through the almost transluscent cuticle and when the first-stage nymphs have taken a meal of blood they are shining red in colour, like 'rubies'. Afterwards the blood darkens and thereafter the gut appears purplish-black. The young nymph is able to feed almost immediately after emergence and thereafter feeds regularly, at least twice daily. The nymph (and the adult) feeds by pressing the front of its head against the skin of its host; a series of curved teeth around the mouth then fasten on to the skin and the piercing stylets are released from a pouch where they are normally invisible, to pierce the skin. Saliva from the salivary glands lubricates the stylets.

Length of life-cycle. The egg hatches in from 8 to 9 days and the nymphal stages take approximately the same length of time. The life-cycle takes place, therefore, every 18 days. The length of the adult stage in the male is 10 days and experimentally the length of the adult stage in the female was found to vary from 9 to 22 days. A maximum of about 57 eggs are laid by each female and the maximum hatch has been found to be 88 per cent. Resistance to starvation is not very great, at 23 °C. the Head Lice die after 55 hours.

Economic importance. Although human lice are known to transmit dangerous diseases, it is the feeling of revulsion and shame when a person becomes aware that he or she is infested with lice which causes anxiety and worry. The bites of the lice cause inflammation and irritation and the scratching which ensues often causes secondary infections, such as impetigo, furunculosis and eczema. It is thought that impetigo in schoolchildren is frequently caused by human louse infection in the first place.

Diseases known to be transmitted by human lice are exanthematic typhus and trench fever (caused by rickettsia), and a relapsing fever caused by a spirochaete. It should be mentioned, however, that epidemics of the above diseases have been transmitted by the Body Louse, not the Head Louse.

Girls and women are more liable to infestation by head lice than are men and boys and head lice infestations are much more frequent than body lice infestations. Children are more prone to infestation than adolescents and adolescents than older people.

The Body Louse, *Pediculus humanis* var *corporis.* (See Fig. 23)

Appearance. The Body Louse is similar to the Head Louse in appearance. In fact a single specimen cannot be differentiated with certainty. In general, however, the Body Louse is from 10 to 20 per cent larger, has thinner antennae, not such deep abdominal indentations but better developed abdominal muscles than the Head Louse. These differences, however, would have to be shown in a large number of specimens as all the characters given above would overlap in the two forms.

Life-cycle

Egg. This again is generally similar to that of the Head Louse. The eggs,

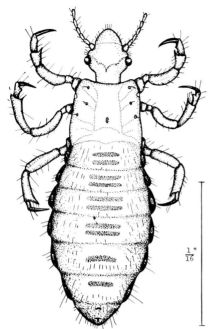

Fig. 23. The Body Louse,
Pediculus humanus var corporis.

$\frac{1}{16}$"

however, are glued to fibres of clothing just as those of the Head Louse are glued to hairs, they are sometimes found stuck to body hairs. Usually most eggs are to be found in the seams of clothes which come in contact with the skin where the adults and the nymphal stages are to be found. The Body Louse lays about twice as many eggs as the Head Louse but the incubation time is the same.

Nymphal stages. These occur just as in the Head Louse but there is a difference in their environment in that the Body Louse nymphs spend the greater part of their time in the clothing, and feeding on the host only takes place when the host is resting or sleeping. All stages of the Body Louse congregate together, being attracted to each other by smell, in which the odour of the excrement plays some part. Body lice crawl about the clothing, generally keeping close to the host's body, although in heavy infestations they may be seen crawling on the outer garments.

Length of life-cycle. Again this is similar to that of the Head Louse, but there are a number of physiological differences between the two forms. The Body Louse can be said to be more robust that the Head Louse, as experimentally it has been found that the adults live about twice as long as head lice, are more resistant to starvation and exhibit less mortality during development.

Economic importance. Modern living standards and greatly improved hygiene have resulted in the Body Louse becoming relatively rare in our homes. But it still occurs amongst vagrants and aged infirm people who exist without proper care and attention, and without regular washing of underwear. During wartime the Body Louse becomes a much larger problem due to lower standards of cleanliness both of the body and the clothing. Transmission of the Body Louse is thought to come about most commonly by an infested person huddling together for warmth with uninfested persons, as occurs in wartime, but infested furniture can also pass on this pest.

The Crab Louse, *Phthirus pubis.* (See Fig. 24)

Appearance. This insect is easily differentiated from the Head Louse and Body Louse by the strong thick claws of its mid- and hind legs, whilst the claws of the fore legs are long and fine. The body is broader than long, contrasting with both varieties of *Pediculus humanus.*

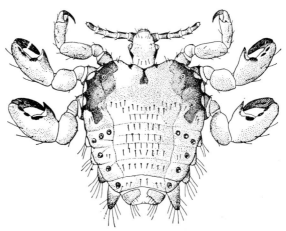

Fig. 24. The Crab Louse, *Phthirus pubis. Reproduced by permission of the Trustees of the British Museum.*

Life-cycle. The egg is slightly smaller than that of *Pediculus* and it is glued to a body hair with more cement than is usual with the last-named insect. The egg hatches in 7 to 8 days. The three nymphal stages do not wander far from the hair, which is grasped with the tarsal claws. Several hours are taken to complete each blood-sucking meal.

The nymphs become adults in from 13 to 17 days and it seems probable that the length of adult life is not more than one month. Fewer eggs are laid than *Pediculus.* The adult is unable to survive longer than 24 hours when removed from its host.

Economic importance. This louse is almost always found clinging to hairs which are stouter and more widely spaced than hairs of the head. Thus the pubic hairs and the peri-anal hairs are those most usually affected although the eyelashes and eyebrows sometimes harbour an infestation. It is generally thought that transmission occurs only during sexual contact, but this is not invariably the case as it is found from time to time on babies.

The Dog Sucking Louse, *Linognathus setosus*. (See Fig. 25)

Appearance. It is not unlike *Pediculus humanus* in general shape although it is somewhat broader across the abdomen, and it lacks eyes. The male is about 1·5 mm. in length and the female a little larger at 2·0 mm.

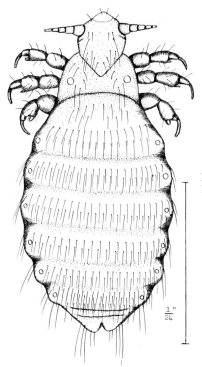

Fig. 25. The Dog Sucking Louse, *Linognathus setosus*.

Life-cycle. Little precise information is available concerning the life-cycle of this pest of long-haired dogs. It usually infests the back, flanks and the base of the tail.

In spite of the irritation, the resulting loss of condition and the lifeless-looking coat, the worst nature of Dog Louse infestation is the insidious maintenance of the dog tapeworm *Dipylidium caninum*. The reproductive broken-off segments of this tapeworm, an internal parasite, are not an uncommon feature of the faeces of dogs and the immature stages of the tapeworm inhabit the body of the biting louse, an external parasite.

6

THE BED BUG

Hemiptera—Heteroptera

The Bed Bug *Cimex lectularius.* (See Plate I)

This human parasite is a member of the order HEMIPTERA. This order is characterized by the members possessing mouth parts which are adapted for piercing and sucking. The lower lip (labium) is modified to form a grooved sheath which receives two pairs of bristle-like stylets, which are the modified mandibles and maxillae. Members of this order are generally characterized by the possession of two pairs of wings, the front pair of which are usually harder in consistency than the hind pair. In the suborder HOMOPTERA, the forewings are more or less uniform but in the suborder HETEROPTERA, the apical part of the fore wing is softer or more membraneous than the rest of the wing.

The HEMIPTERA include a number of widely different forms from the aphids on the one hand to the water scorpions on the other, but the vast majority are suckers of plant sap. Many species are carriers of important plant diseases and thus are of the widest significance to man's economy. A few species, however, in the family CIMICIDAE and related families are suckers of mammalian and bird blood and it is to the named family that the Bed Bug belongs.

Appearance. Bed Bugs are round, flat insects of a rich reddish brown 'mahogany' colour, which has led to their being called 'Mahogany Flats'. The legs are well developed and they can crawl up vertical surfaces of wood, paper and plaster, and, with a little more difficulty, dirty glass. They are unable to crawl up clean glass or other polished, smooth surfaces. They are almost wingless, the forewings are represented by small vestigial scales, the hindwings are absent altogether. The antennae are easily seen and the first two segments appear to be angled. The compound eyes are also visible and are cone-like consisting of about 30 facets. Males may easily be distinguished from females by the end of the abdomen terminating in a rather sharp flap-like segment, whilst in the female it is rounded.

Life-cycle. (See Fig. 8)

The egg. The female Bed Bug lays her eggs in cracks and crevices in the vicinity of the host and in doing so they are covered with glue which

64

cements them firmly in position. The total number of eggs laid by one female at 25°C. and with frequent feeding, say two feeds per week, is about 345. The eggs have been described as being like the rubber bulbs of a fountain-pen filler and they measure from 0·8 to 1·3 mm. in length and from 0·4 to 0·6 mm. in width. The cap, which drops off on hatching, is well defined 'like a manhole cover'. Unhatched eggs are easily identified from hatched ones, the former being opaque and pearly in colour, whilst the latter are translucent and opalescent. It has been found experimentally that the period of incubation varies from 5·5 days to 28°C. to 48·7 days at 13°C.

Nymphal stages. The five nymphal stages all resemble the adult as shown in the illustration except that the cuticle, being not so thick, shows the state of digestion of the enclosed blood meal. Each nymphal stage requires one full meal of blood before it proceeds to the next stage, and as the amount of blood taken at each meal is from 2½ to 6 times the original weight of the Bed Bug, it can be imagined that the size of the bugs varies greatly. The average sizes for each stage have been given as follows: I 1·3 mm., II 2·0 mm., III 3·0 mm., IV 3·7 mm.

Length of life-cycle. At normal room temperature (18°C.–20°C.) and provided there is unlimited opportunity for feeding, the adult bug may live from 9 to 18 months. At higher temperatures than this, length of the adult life is shorter, being about 15 weeks at 27°C. and only about 10 weeks at 34°C. At lower temperatures than normal Bed Bugs become more sluggish, whilst at 90°C. they will not move to seek their host.

There are figures available for the length of the complete life-cycle at various temperatures. Thus at 28°C. the complete life-cycle is passed through in 34 days. At 25°C. it is 46 days, at 23°C. it is 61 days. At 18°C. the life-cycle is completed in 125 days and at 15°C. it is completed in 237 days. At 13°C. the life-cycle is not completed.

Bed Bugs exhibit considerable resistance to starvation. At 23°C. this figure is 85 days for males and 69 days for females, whilst at 13°C., the temperature at which the life-cycle is not completed, both sexes of Bed Bugs can live for about a year without feeding. One case has been observed in which a female lived for 565 days without feeding.

Bed Bugs are resistant, to a fair degree, to exposure to low temperatures. Only a quarter of the individuals are killed when exposed to −17°C. for one hour, but a higher proportion of eggs die during prolonged winter temperatures of 0 to 9°C.

Economic importance. The Bed Bug is likely to be found in any premises where low hygienic standards prevail, such as in slum property. Almost always it is the bedroom which is infested. Over-crowded, dirty rooms may support large numbers of bugs which hide in crevices in woodwork and plaster and under loose wallpaper. From these situations, the bugs search out a suitable host at night and cause irritation and thus loss of sleep to most human beings that they 'bite'. Some people, on the other

E

hand, seem oblivious to their attentions. They are not known to transmit disease, but are, however, looked upon with loathing and abhorrence by all who come into contact with them, especially as a disgusting odour is usually associated with them. The bugs possess stink glands which operate when the insects are disturbed. The usual method by which Bed Bugs enter a house is through the introduction of infested bedroom furniture or suitcases, although they are also carried around on outer clothing, such as overcoats and hats, which have been hung against an infested wall. In addition, their flat bodies facilitate their entry into adjacent bedrooms in terraced property through cracks in poorly constructed brickwork and ill-fitting joinery. The general elevation of hygiene standards during recent years has resulted in the Bed Bug being less common than it was formerly.

7

LACEWINGS AND MOTHS

Green Lacewing, Clothes and House Moths

Neuroptera and *Lepidoptera*

The ENDOPTERYGOTA or HOLOMETABOLA
We shall now consider those insect pests of the household belonging to this more highly developed group. They are all characterized by the wings developing internally, by the presence of a larval stage which differs considerably in form from the adult, and by a pupal stage which again shows important differences when compared with the adult. This is known as a complete or complex metamorphosis.

The Green Lacewing, *Chrysopa carnea.* (See Fig. 26)
This insect belongs to the order NEUROPTERA or PLANIPENNIA of which only 54 species are found in Britain. Members of this order are characterized by having soft bodies, elongated antennae, mouth parts adapted for biting and the two pairs of similar membraneous wings are held tent-wise over the body when the insect is at rest. The larvae are carnivorous with either biting or suctorial mouth parts. Several species, of which that named above is the most common, are likely to be found indoors.

Appearance. The richly veined (hence name Lacewing) green or greenish yellow wings folded over the body, the large compound eyes sometimes shining bronze in colour are characters sufficient to identify this insect.

Life-cycle. The eggs, which are laid singly, are borne on long slender stalks. The larva is torpedo-shaped with many bristles arising from tubercles scattered over the body, and the jaws are sickle-shaped and pointed. They feed on any soft-bodied insects and mites that they can seize with their jaws, but aphids constitute their usual prey.

Economic importance. Lacewings are important beneficial insects in agriculture and forestry on account of the number of aphids they consume. A related species is recorded as destroying 300 to 400 aphids during its larval life. In Britain, the species mentioned above enters dwellings fortuitously when seeking a site for hibernation. Sometimes when adjacent to deciduous woodlands many specimens may enter bedrooms in the autumn, but they are entirely innocuous.

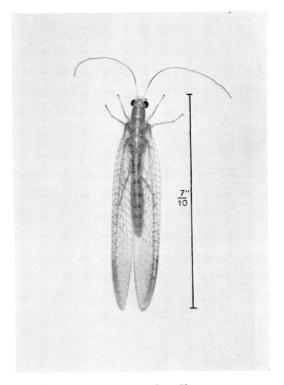

Fig. 26. The Green Lacewing, *Chrysopa carnea.*

CLOTHES MOTHS AND HOUSE MOTHS

Moths (and butterflies) are classified in the insect order LEPIDOPTERA, which literally means the scaly-winged insects. This is an important characteristic of moths, indeed not only the two pairs of wings, but the body and legs are covered with hair-like or powder-like scales. The mouth parts are very specialized, with the mandibles absent and the maxillae modified to fit together to form a sucking tube or *proboscis.* The Clothes and House Moths do not eat or consume any material during their adult life, but live on good reserves laid down during their larval life. The larvae are long and cylindrical and in addition to the six thoracic legs bear five pairs of false feet or prolegs on the abdomen. There are said to be about 100,000 species in this order of insects of which about 2000 are found in Britain (see Plate II).

Origin of wool-feeding habit. Before civilized man, the wool- and fur-eating larvae of moths (and also some species of beetles) inhabited old birds' nests and lairs of carnivorous animals. Here they subsisted on the fur, hair and feathers used in the nests of the birds or on the pieces of skin left about when finished with by the carnivore. When man started to use fur and wool for his clothing the scavenging moth larvae followed, when they were able to utilize to a greater extent fur and wool soiled with natural secretions or with urine and faecal matter. Under present-day conditions, although Clothes and House Moth larvae are able to complete their development feeding on clean wool and fur, they show a decided preference to spots on clothing soiled by spilled foodstuffs, perspiration or urine.

Classification of Clothes Moths and House Moths. The three species of Clothes Moths which we consider in the chapter are classified in the family TINAEIDAE and the House Moths in the family OECOPHORIDAE. Representatives of these two families may be easily identified by examining the way in which the wings are held when at rest. The Clothes Moths hold the wings tent-wise, forming an angle over the abdomen. The House Moths, on the other hand, hold their wings almost flat and rather scissor-like. It should be noted that in addition to the Clothes Moths and House Moths found in a high proportion of our homes, certain species of moths are important pests of stored foods including grain and grain products, cocoa and dried fruit, but these are pests rather of food manufacturing establishments and warehouses and now seldom find their way into our dwellings.

The Common Clothes Moth, *Tineola bisselliella.* (See Plate II)

Appearance. The upper-side of the forewings, i.e. that part of the wings seen when the insect is at rest, are of a pale ochreous buff, almost a golden colour and appear in certain lights to glitter like gold. There are no spots or marks on the wings and there is no 'dusting' of dark scales. The length of the insect, when it is at rest, from the top of the head to the end of the wings is about 6 to 8 mm. The head is covered with long silky hairs which make it appear rather larger. There is a fringe of long hairs around the borders of the wings. It prefers, however, to run rather than fly and it is said that those seen in flight are males or spent females.

Life-cycle

The egg. These are oval, just over 0·5 mm. in length and 0·3 mm. wide. They are slightly sticky when first laid but although there is some adhesion to suitable substances they do not stick firmly. The adult female will lay her eggs whether they have been fertilized or not, but only those fertilized will hatch. She usually lays them all within three days. At 15°C. the eggs hatch in 24 days, at 20°C., 10 days, at 25°C., 7 days, and at 30°C., 6 days. Hatching occurs when the embryo larva, which has been occupying a U position in the egg, bites its way out of the egg. The total number of eggs laid varies from 50 to 100.

The larva. This is a caterpillar, creamy white in colour with the head golden brown. No eyes are visible but nevertheless it is able to crawl away from the light to hide itself. There are six thoracic legs, each terminating in a claw. Five abdominal segments each bear a pair of fleshy prolegs, those on the last abdominal segment being somewhat larger and are known as the 'claspers'. At the base of each proleg there is a circlet of small hooks or crochets which enable the larva to walk firmly over a variety of substances. In order to walk vertically up a polished surface such as glass, however, the larva secretes a silken pad which sticks to the smooth surface and allows the legs to obtain a firm grasp. Silk is secreted from large glands in the thorax and head of the larva and emerges (or rather is extruded) from the spinneret, a tube-like organ situated on the under-side of the head.

Fig. 27. Damage to woollen fabric by Clothes Moth larva.

The larva is not usually visible during its day-to-day activities as it constructs a loose, open-ended, web-like gallery in which it is normally found. The larva moults at least four times and each time constructs a strong silken cocoon in which the moult takes place. When the larva hatches from the egg it measures about 1 mm. in length but when fully grown is about 10 mm. in length. The fairly large, light coloured faecal pellets are often a feature of an infestation and they are often mistaken by the householder for eggs.

Pupa. The pupa of the Common Clothes Moth bears a general similarity to the usual moth pupa or chrysalis. It is reddish brown in colour and its form is known as 'obtect', that is, the appendages are all adherent to the body and the pupal cuticle is thick and leathery. However, the tips of the wings and legs are free at their extremities and in addition the abdominal segments are more mobile than is the usual case with moth pupae. It measures up to 7 mm. in length. When examining infestations of Common Clothes Moths, it is usual to see the old pupal skins protruding from the cocoons, to which point the pupa has wriggled before the emergence has taken place. The old skins can easily be identified on account of their flimsy dull nature and the line of rupture around the antennae. Living pupae, on the other hand, are bright and shiny, heavy, and, of course, show no lines of rupture.

The adult moth lives 2 to 3 weeks. Provided favourable conditions exist there is an annual life-cycle, but there may be two or even more in the year.

Economic importance. The Common Clothes Moth is said to be by far the most serious pest of clothes and furnishing fabrics in Britain and it is ubiquitous. The larvae feed on all materials, clothes and textiles of animal origin but can also damage other textiles by biting and discarding the fibres. In textiles of mixed origin such as those containing cotton and woollen fibres, the threads of the latter may be severed and thus give a 'cat-scratching' effect. There have been surveys and estimates of the national cost of moth damage (although this would include Carpet Beetle damage) and in 1948 it was estimated that damage to the extent of £1·5 million was caused. That was of course, estimated at 1948 prices; at present-day prices the figure would be about £2·5 millions. It is interesting to note that in the 1948 survey (Social Survey of the Central Office of Information) 26 per cent of the sample of households had suffered moth damage during the previous 15 months, 30 per cent considered moth damage a serious problem but 80 per cent took some precautions against moths.

The Case-Bearing Clothes Moth, *Tinaea pellionella.* (See Plate II)

Appearance. The upper-side of the forewings (that part of the wings visible when the moth is at rest) are pale shining buff or brown in colour with three rather faint dark spots. There is a slight dusting of dark scales which gives it a rather darker and duller appearance than the Common Clothes Moth.

Life-cycle

Egg. This can be identified from that of the previous species by the surface structure, which can be seen only by a strong lens or the low power of a microscope. In the case-bearer, longitudinal ridges can be made out whereas in the previous species the ridges assume a reticulate pattern.

Larva. The larva is more easily identified by its case which gives it its common name. This is of characteristic shape as shown in the Plate. It is open at each end and the larva drags it about with it wherever it goes. The first few segments of the larva only are visible. It can support the case, even though with difficulty, when climbing up a vertical wall. It is usually to be found, however, around carpets and heavy woollen curtains that are little disturbed. The main part of the case is constructed of silk but attached to it are cut-off fibres of wool and various detritus so that the case usually assumes the colour of the material which the larva is infesting and which often makes their detection difficult by the householder. The larvae never leave their cases and when ready to pupate do so only after sealing both ends.

Pupa. This is only to be found inside the larval/pupal case although when ready to emerge the pupa forces its way through the thin silk membrane before the pupal skin ruptures and the moth emerges.

Economic importance. This species is nothing like so important as the previous species but even so is responsible for considerable damage. In a large number of cases it escapes detection due to the habit of the larva.

Tapestry Moth or White-Tip Clothes Moth, *Trichophaga tapetzella*

Appearance. When at rest this moth closely resembles a bird dropping. The basal third of the forewing is white with the tip of the wing shading darker. The white part of the wing may be mottled to a greater or lesser extent and the front of the head is also covered with white hairs.

This species is the largest of the Clothes Moths and measures from 22 to 25 mm. across the wings, and when at rest the male is about 8·5 mm. and the female about 10·5 mm. in length.

Life-cycle. The biology of this moth has not been studied to the same extent as have the other species of wool-destroying moths. In a room maintained at 65° F. all stages may be present throughout the year.

Larva. The larvae of this species are said normally to infest coarser materials than the other Clothes Moths, examples being horsehair, stuffings and skins. It is more usually to be found in sheds, barns and outhouses than in dwellings, and the larvae, which construct rough silken tunnels in the infested materials, grow to about 14 mm. in length. Although the inside of the tunnels is smooth, the outside is to some extent camouflaged with faecal pellets, bits of fibre and hair and other material which has been bitten off by the larvae.

Pupa. A cocoon is formed of tough silk and the pupa makes its way partly out of it before the adult emerges. The empty pupal cases (as in the other species of Clothes Moth) protruding from the infested material are a feature of an infestation.

Economic importance. This species is not nearly so common in houses as the previous two species. Its name of Tapestry Moth refers to its being able to attack heavier and coarser materials. It is more likely to be found infesting materials of wool and hair that have been discarded and have laid undisturbed for some considerable time without attention in a shed or barn probably in rather humid conditions.

The Brown House Moth, *Hofmannophila pseudospretella.* (See Plate II)

Appearance. Head, thorax and forewings brown, the general background colour varying from dark olive-brown to a lighter buff. The thorax and forewings are speckled with dark flecks in a variable manner, but on each forewing there are several large spots. Across the wings the male measures from 17 to 19 mm., whilst the female measures from about 18 to over 25 mm. When at rest the male measures about 8·5 mm. whilst the female measures about 14·4 mm. in length. When disturbed, it runs quickly to hide in dark folds or crevices, and in fact, like the preceding species, those seen actually flying are most likely to be males or spent females.

Life-cycle. Little experimental work has been carried out on this and the following species. It certainly requires to be done.

Larva. This reaches a length of 18 to 20 mm. and in colour is shining white, with the head and a plate on the first thoracic segment bright chestnut. The larva spins very little silk when feeding on wool and feathers, in contrast with the Common Clothes Moth. When feeding on loose friable materials, however, such as chicken meal or farinaceous meals of various sorts, a little more silk is produced. The range of materials which this insect will infest is wide and varied. From general accounts it appears that, some years ago, it relied more on substances of vegetable origin such as seeds, dried plants and dried fruits, than perhaps is the case today, although it still remains a grave menace to the corks of wine-bottles stored in damp cellars in France. Woollen carpets and upholstered furniture are often attacked by this species, the fat naked-looking larvae hiding under the carpet edge or in the deep pockets of chairs and sofas. The phenomenon of *diapause* is exhibited by this species. This is the ability of the larva to tide over a period of unfavourable conditions by assuming a resting, non-active condition. It spins a thin but tough cocoon and lives upon its reserve food material. This may occur during very cold weather but it often takes place for unaccountable reasons. It is thought that sometimes an inherited rhythmic periodicity may provoke diapause. At the end of diapause, the larva bites its way out of the cocoon and recommences feeding.

Pupa. Before pupation a tough silken torpedo-shaped cocoon is constructed, usually in a fold of the infested material. The length of the pupal stage is said to be about 10 days.

Economic importance. There is a certain amount of controversy concerning the importance of the Brown House Moth as a pest in buildings. Certainly for the years immediately following the Second World War it appeared to the writer from the numbers of specimens of the larvae sent in for identification (in the mistaken belief that they were woodworms) to be equal or nearly equal in importance to the Common Clothes Moth. However, there is no doubt that it plays an important role in the household as a pest of almost any material of animal origin which remains undisturbed and slightly damp. To the usual materials must be added leather used in upholstery and bookbinding. Occasionally it will be found attacking materials of vegetable origin, such as various foodstuffs left overlong in tins in the pantry, and even cork mats.

The White-Shouldered House Moth, *Endrosis sarcitrella* (sometimes given as *lactella*). (See Plate II)

Appearance. The head and the front of the thorax is white, the white part of the thorax giving a cape-like effect. The forewings are greyish or greyish-brown, mottled with darker and lighter tones. The length from head to tip of wings, in the resting position, in the male is 6 mm. whilst the female is 10·5 mm. Across the wings, from wing-tip to wing-tip, the male measures up to about 14·5 mm., whilst the female measures from 17 mm. to over 19.5 mm. It is this species which is often encountered by the housewife when it has dropped into a jug of milk or water left overnight and its struggles on the surface are evident by the trail of scales which are left. (The milk-jug habit obviously inspired the specific name *lactella* which was used at one time.) The adult may be seen from May to October.

Life-cycle. Little work has been carried out on the biology of this insect so that what we know of it has been derived largely from random observation.

Larva. The larva grows to about 13 mm. in length and is ivory white in colour. The larvae are to be found all the year round and damage much the same range of material as does the Brown House Moth.

Economic importance. Although widely distributed and commonly found throughout the British Isles, it never assumes the importance as a pest of the preceding species. When the two species are found together, as is sometimes the case, the Brown House Moth always predominates.

PARASITES AND PREDATORS

Two parasites of the Clothes Moths may often be observed in the home, first the little braconid *Spathius exarator* may be seen walking rapidly over window-panes. It is dark in colour and the long bristle-like egg-laying tube of the female is easily made out. The predacious larva of the window fly *Scenopinus fenestralis* attacks the larvae of Clothes Moths and House Moths and eats them. This species is described in Chapter 10.

8

BEETLES

Wood-boring Beetles—Mealworm Beetle—Spider Beetles—Plaster Beetles—Larder Beetle—Carpet Beetles and other beetles

Coleoptera

In this chapter, pests of the home which are classified in the order COLEOP-TERA are described. These are the beetles which are usually readily identified by the first pair of wings being highly modified and adapted to form hard, horny wing covers or wing cases—known as the elytra—which cover and protect the second pair of wings which are membraneous and are folded up beneath them. The functional wings are thus invisible unless the insect is actually flying or preparing for flight. Many beetles, however, lack wings entirely. Beetles are further characterized by the prothorax being large and to some extent movable and by the mouth parts being adapted for biting. There is a complete metamorphosis and the larvae show a very wide range of forms and habits.

There are about a quarter of a million different species of beetles which constitute the largest order in the animal kingdom. About 3,700 different species are found in Britain and it is thus understandable that beetles have become adapted to fit themselves into a very wide range of environments and to utilize a similar wide variety of substances as foodstuffs. It has been thought that the hard, well-fitting exoskeleton has been an important factor in their evolution as the dominant insect order on the earth.

The first group which we describe in this chapter consume wood for their nutrition.

THE WOOD-BORING BEETLES

Although a large number of beetles have been recorded as emerging from wood indoors we shall deal here with the seven species most commonly met with. Wood showing unsightly holes through which the wood-boring beetles have emerged is said to be *worm-eaten* and the immature boring stage of the beetle, the larval stage, is referred to as *woodworm*.

The first two species are classified in the family ANOBIIDAE

Common Furniture Beetle *Anobium punctatum.* (See Plate III)

Appearance. This is a 'small brown beetle' varying in length from 2·5 to 6 mm. Although usually chocolate-brown in colour, lighter and darker individuals occur. One of the most characteristic features by which this species may be identified is the almost vertical insertion of the head into the prothorax which latter is thereby given a hood-like shape. This results in making the head invisible when viewed from the top. The wing cases bear a number of longitudinal rows of small pits which appear darker in colour. The whole of the insect is covered with short golden hairs, which, however, can only be seen with a lens of high power. The beetle can fly well but those usually found flying are males. The females prefer to hide in old flight-holes.

Life-cycle

The egg. The ellipsoidal eggs are whitish in colour and measure 0·55 mm. in length and 0·35 mm. in width. Usually the female lays from 20 to 60 eggs but the average is said to be about 28. The maximum number of eggs produced in the ovaries is 80. They are laid in small groups of 2, 3 or 4, wedged in cracks, crevices or joints in unpainted and unpolished wood and sometimes pushed just inside old flight-holes.

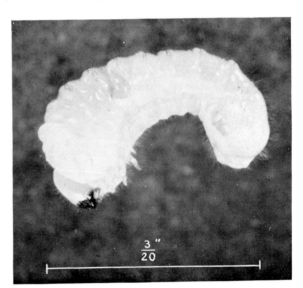

Fig. 28. Larva of *Anobium punctatum*.

$$\frac{3}{20}''$$

The larva. The larva eats its way through the bottom of the egg-shell and thus enters the crack in which the egg has been inserted. It then commences to bore into the wood. The whole of the larval life takes place in the wood so that a larva will not be observed unless the infested wood is broken open. The number of larval moults does not appear to have been studied. The larva grows to a length of about 7 mm. and is greyish-white in colour. Except in the first stage, it is strongly arched or 'crescentic' in shape, the thoracic segments being the larger but the last segment is enlarged also (see Fig. 28). The legs, although small, are of five segments and are well developed. The head is almost circular and yellow in colour. The larva mostly tunnels up and down the grain but from time to time crossing over into a different growth-ring. The tunnel or gallery is loosely filled with powdery bore dust or frass. This consists of rejected wood fibres and faecal pellets. The latter are barrel shaped and give the bore dust a gritty feel when rubbed between the fingers.

When the larva is mature it directs the gallery towards the outside of the wood in a straight line and immediately beneath the wood surface constructs a pupal chamber rather larger in diameter than the larval tunnel. Here, after a short period in a 'prepupal' phase, it changes to a pupa.

The pupa. The creamy-white pupa resembles the adult beetle in shape but it is soft and the appendages, legs, antennae, wing cases and wings, although visible, are held down by the thin transparent pupal skin. It can move only the last few segments of the abdomen. When ready to emerge the pupal skin is burst longitudinally down the upper part of the thorax and, after a few days, when the exoskeleton is hard, the adult bites its way out. Whilst doing this it rotates and thus the exit or flight-hole is perfectly circular. It is about 1/16 in. in diameter.

Length of life-cycle. Anobium punctatum has been shown to be a difficult insect to culture under controlled conditions so that precise information on the length of the different life-stages is not yet available. The egg hatches at normal room temperatures in between two and three weeks. The total length of the life-cycle probably averages between three and four years and is never less than two years, although out of doors an annual life-cycle is said to take place. The pupal stage is said to last from 6 to 8 weeks.

Economic importance. Common Furniture Beetle is one of the most important insect pests found in buildings in Britain. An active infestation by this insect is believed to occur in something between 50 and 80 per cent of the 16½ million dwellings in Britain. Such an infestation lowers the value of a property by an average of about £100. It is estimated that the present annual cost of *in situ* treatments is £10 m., and it is certain that this figure will grow, as it does not appear to have caught up with the increase in the rate of distribution of the pest during recent years. Common Furniture Beetle is a common insect out of doors where it is found attacking dead wood still attached to a living tree, such as branch scars or where bark has been rubbed off, thus killing the underlying sapwood. Such situations are almost always found to be peppered with the flight-holes of *Anobium punctatum*. The attacked wood is most usually found to be a hardwood such as oak or fruit trees, yet indoors it is mainly a softwood pest, found in rafters and purlins in the roof void, and joists, flooring and joinery of the ground and first floor. Yet its name *furniture* beetle denotes that formerly it was more important as a pest of furniture (which is mainly of hardwood). Even so, it severely attacks birch plywood (see Fig. 29), commonly used as a backing for furniture, and also wickerwork, which is

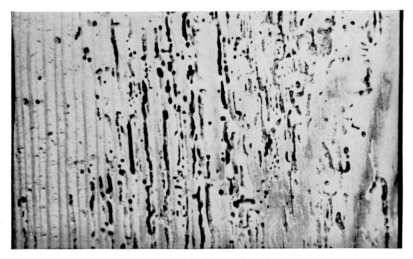

Fig. 29. Wood damaged by larvae of *Anobium punctatum.*

made from the peeled twigs of willow. Although the beetle can fly well, it has been thought more recently that its present wide distribution has been brought about by the movement of furniture. It has been estimated that 800,000 homes change hands each year so that it is not hard to see that furniture with woodworm infested backing introduced into a non-infested house would provide an annual hazard at each flight season.

PARASITES AND PREDATORS

Furniture Beetle larvae are sometimes found to be attacked by small mites called *Pyemotes ventricosus* which appear on the larvae like small shining pearls. They suck the juices of the larva until it finally shrivels away. Another parasite is the small wingless chalcid wasp which looks like a small black ant. This is known as *Theocolax formiciformis*, the female of which lays her eggs on the back of the host larva or near to it. On hatching the parasitic larvae consume the beetle larva. The adults bore their own way out of the wood.

Sometimes, in the vicinity of a heavy infestation of Furniture Beetle (and Death Watch Beetle too, see later), a shining steely-blue beetle is encountered; this is named *Korynetes caeruleus*, both the adult and the larvae of which prey upon the larvae of woodworm. The larva of this predator is rather like the larva of the Brown House Moth but it can be differentiated from the latter by the possession of a pair of horn-like processes on the hinder extremity of the body. It moves slowly round the woodworm galleries consuming the larvae when it encounters them.

Death Watch Beetle, *Xestobium rufovillosum*

Appearance. This insect is much larger than the Common Furniture Beetle, measuring just over one-quarter of an inch in length; the females are usually the larger, and particularly large specimens may be up to one-third of an inch long. In colour it is dark greyish-brown with a pattern of patches of yellow scale-like hairs on the pronotum and wing cases. The yellow patches, however, are quickly lost when the insect becomes rubbed and it then has a reddish, shining appearance. There are no longitudinal rows of pits on the wing cases as are present on *Anobium punctatum*. The pronotum is large, helmet shaped with large lateral flanges. Only very rarely has Death Watch been known to fly so that it is always found near the wood which it is infesting, or where it has dropped on to the floor if it is attacking timber in a roof. The size of the flight-hole through which the adult insect emerges from the wood is about $\frac{1}{8}$ in. in diameter. The tapping noise made by both sexes of the adult beetles is a well-known phenomenon and, heard in the quiet hours of the night, in a sick room, has given rise to its common name. The tapping is made by striking the head against the wood on which it is standing.

Life-cycle

The egg. Small clusters of 3 or 4 eggs are laid on the surface of rough wood, in cracks or just inside flight holes. When first laid they are sticky and adhere to each other. They are whitish and oval in shape and measure about 0.65×0.45 mm. The average number of eggs laid is between 40 and 60 and the maximum number recorded is 201.

The larva. The creamy-white strongly hook-shaped larva is similar in general appearance to that of the Common Furniture Beetle. If examined with a lens it is seen to be covered with short, erect golden hairs and there are two black eye spots on each side of the head, compared with only one on the larva of *Anobium punctatum*. On hatching there is a difference in behaviour between the two species. Whereas the larvae of the Furniture Beetle, finding themselves already in a crack, commence to bore into it straightaway, the larvae of Death Watch wander about in an agile manner before selecting the precise crevice or old flight-hole in which they will commence to bore. The larva grows to a length of almost half an inch and the frass is characterized by the presence of bun-shaped pellets easily identified with the naked eye.

Pupa. Very much like that of the Furniture Beetle but larger. It is to be found in a pupal chamber immediately beneath the wood surface.

Length of life-cycle. This is very variable but is thought to average between 4 and 5 years. Under the best possible condition for this species the life-cycle takes place in one year; on the other hand, lengths of life-cycle of ten years and over are known. The egg stage lasts from two to five weeks according to conditions. There is some doubt concerning the length of the pupal stage but it is generally thought that the larva changes to a pupa in late summer, remains in this stage for three or four weeks only, metamorphoses into the adult and remains within the pupal chamber until the following early spring. It normally emerges from the latter part of April to the beginning of May.

Economic importance. Death Watch Beetle is of some considerable importance as a pest of wooden structures in older buildings in Britain. It is most common in the south of England but from the Midlands it becomes progressively rarer northwards and is absent from Scotland. It is known from only two localities in Ireland. It attacks hardwoods such as oak and chestnut and always where some fungal decay has taken or is taking place.

It is most usual for Death Watch attacks to originate in timber of large dimensions and it is thought that the actual introduction of the pest into the buildings took place at the time of construction. The timber was of such large cross-section that it was inevitably taken from over-mature trees already containing pockets of rot in which Death Watch larvae were concealed. Such timber has not been used in building for many years so that it seems certain that few new Death Watch attacks now occur. Those being dealt with now by the servicing companies mean that the total number of infestations indoors is decreasing.

Death Watch is a common insect out of doors being found in dead wood, branches or trunks of a number of hardwood trees, where fungal decay has commenced. A common situation for it is in the decaying crown or trunk of old pollard willows. It can conceivably be brought indoors in such wood cut up for fire-logs, and emerging beetles could initiate an attack if they found decaying or partially decayed wood on which to lay their eggs.

The Wood-Boring Weevils, *Euophryum confine* and *Pentarthrum huttoni.* (See Fig. 30)

These are classified in the family CURCULIONIDAE

Although two species are given here it is virtually (but not absolutely) certain that what is said below concerning the growing importance of wood-boring weevils relates to the first-named species. The two species, however, are so similar in appearance that they can be separated only by a trained entomologist.

Appearance. These insects are typical weevils with a long cylindrical body, pear-shaped pronotum and the head bearing a long *rostrum* or snout half-way along which arise the elbowed antennae. They vary in length from $\frac{1}{10}$ to $\frac{1}{5}$ in. *E. confine* is, on the average, a little smaller than *P. huttoni.* The former is blackish-brown to reddish brown and the latter species is more blackish and not nearly so reddish. Flight-holes in infested wood are characterized by their oval shape with jagged or indistinct edges.

PLATE I, opposite: 1. Silverfish, 2. House Cricket, 3. German Cockroach, 4. Bed Bug.

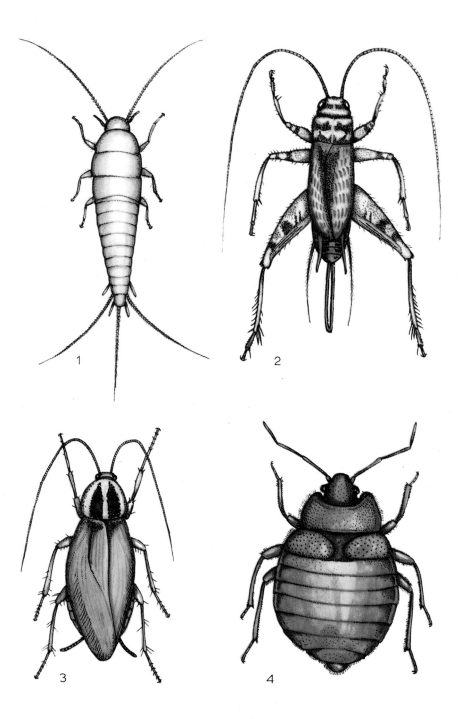

1
2
3
4

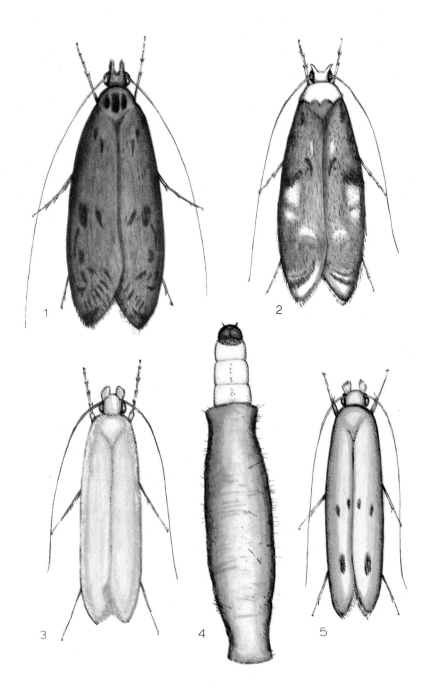

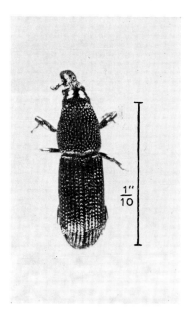

Fig. 30. The Wood-Boring Weevil,
Euophryum confine.

Life-cycle. Only the biology of *P. huttoni* has been studied so that what information is given below relates to this species.

Eggs. The female bites holes in the wood and deposits a single shining white egg in each. The eggs are covered with a semi-transparent whitish excretion. Two females were seen to lay 50 eggs during a period of 80 days.

Larva. The young larva first consumes the whole of the shell then burrows into the wood parallel to the surface. The bore dust is finer in texture and the individual granules are more circular than that of *Anobium punctatum.* The galleries also are smaller and usually less distinct. Five larval instars occur. It is entirely legless and grows to about 3·3 mm. in length. It is nearly white in colour, strongly curved and is widest at about the third thoracic segment. The terminal segment of the abdomen is not enlarged as in *A. punctatum.*

Pupa. The pupal chamber becomes lined with fungal hyphae. The white pupa is about 3·5 mm. in length and is furnished with a pair of strong spines which emerge from fleshy processes situated on the ninth abdominal segment.

Length of life-cycle. The eggs hatch after 16 days and the larva pupates in from 6 to 8 months after hatching. The pupal stage lasts about 16 days.

PLATE II, opposite: 1. Brown House Moth, 2. White-Shouldered House Moth, 3. Common Clothes Moth, 4. Larva of Case-bearing Clothes Moth, 5. Case-bearing Clothes Moth.

F

An important feature of the life-cycle, however, is the length of adult life which is about 16 months. Many weevils living in decaying wood are able to mate within the wood, without requiring to emerge from the wood at the end of each generation. The extent to which this phenomenon is applicable to this species is not known but the adult weevils are able to bore considerable distances.

Economic importance. The wood-boring weevils are found attacking a variety of timbers, both hardwoods and softwoods, which are already partially fungally decayed. Plywood of birch, alder or oak if used as panelling in a damp situation is commonly infested. Flooring blocks, if badly laid with regard to dampness, are often attacked. The associated fungus is almost always the cellar fungus *Coniophora cerebella*, which causes a wet rot.

It is remarkable to note that *E. confine* was not recorded in Britain until 1937 but since that time has become exceedingly common, especially in London and the Home Counties. It is interesting to note also that wet rot is especially common in this area.

Formerly, it was thought that small patches of wet rot in a house were of no significance as long as it was allowed to dry out. Today, wherever the wood-boring weevils occur this is no longer the case.

House Longhorn Beetle, *Hylotrupes bajulus*

This beetle is classified in the very large family CERAMBYCIDAE, almost all of whose members are wood-borers, attacking the living tree or timber either sound or in some stage of decay. Almost every tree species may have one or more species of cerambycid beetles attacking it.

Appearance. Males of this species are often not much more than a quarter of an inch in length whilst females may be as much as one inch. In colour this beetle is greyish-black to a dark brownish-black with two greyish transverse marks across the wing cases. Almost the whole of the body is covered with greyish or yellowish-grey hair. Two areas on the pronotum, however, are quite bare of hair and are shining. They have the appearance of eyes. The antennae are long but not unduly so.

Life-cycle.

Eggs. The greyish-white eggs are spindle-shaped, 1·2 to 2·0 mm. in length and about 0·5 mm. broad. They are laid in clutches in crevices in the wood of the type caused by shrinkage. The average number of eggs laid is between 140 and 200 whilst the maximum number of eggs known to be laid by one female is 582.

Larva. The fleshy, shining, ivory-white larva is generally cylindrical but somewhat flattened. It is broadest in the thoracic region then gradually tapers towards the hinder end before broadening again three segments from the end. The head is small and the hinder part is invaginated into the prothorax but the jaws are large and powerful. The intersegmental grooves are deep. The legs are well defined but small. It reaches a length of 24 mm. and a maximum breadth of 7·5 mm. The young larvae, at first, keep near the outer surface of the wood, the sapwood. This is the area of greatest nutrient value and they grow fast, but as they tunnel deeper into the wood, the rate of growth slows down. The larval galleries are oval in cross-section and are filled with frass consisting of rejected wood fragments and cylindrical faecal pellets. The course of a gallery can often be detected just under the surface of wood by a long blister-like protrusion and sometimes the outer veneer of wood bursts along one of these galleries, showing a long sinuous line of light coloured frass on the surface of the dusty joist. During warm weather when the larvae are most active the noise of their jaws scraping the wood can be heard quite clearly.

Pupa. The white pupa measures up to 25 mm. in length. Although they are more usually found near the surface of the wood, they may occur deeper, even as much as 4 to 6 inches from the surface. Pupation usually takes place in May although it sometimes occurs in autumn and even in winter.

Length of life-cycle. The total length of the life-cycle, of which the greater part is represented by the larval stage, is usually from 3 to 6 years but 2 years and up to 10 years are not uncommon and the maximum recorded is 32 years. The eggs hatch in $5\frac{1}{2}$ to 10 days according to temperature and humidity. The duration of the pupal stage varies from 11 days to $22\frac{1}{2}$ days but the adult remains in the pupal chamber for a few days for the hardening of the integument before it bites its way out of its oval flight hole.

Economic importance. The House Longhorn Beetle is a pest of softwood. Taking Europe as a whole it is a most serious pest of softwood structural timber, but in Britain it is important only in a relatively small area of north-west Surrey. In this area, however, it is probable that something like 50 per cent of all buildings are infested. The attack usually starts and, indeed, may be confined to the roof void. The sapwood is first consumed but later the heartwood may be attacked.

Old, inactive damage is sometimes found in parts of the country other than Surrey but it is thought that the general climatic factors are unsuitable for it elsewhere. It often reaches this country in the larval stage, in orange boxes.

Powder Post Beetle *Lyctus brunneus.* (See Plate III)

Six species of the genus *Lyctus* occur in Britain but *Lyctus brunneus* is by far the most common and the following account will refer only to this species. It is classified in the family LYCTIDAE of which the British native species *Lyctus linearis* is now comparatively uncommon. *L. brunneus* was probably imported from North America.

Appearance. Lyctus brunneus is a long cylindrical beetle, without the 'hooding' of the head as shown by Common Furniture Beetle and Death Watch Beetle. The length is variable, depending very much upon the nutrition of the larva and lengths from 2 to 7 mm. have been recorded. The colour varies too: although a rich reddish chestnut brown is the characteristic colour, much darker specimens are often found. The pronotum is usually darker in colour than the wing cases. Like Common Furntiture Beetle, a number of longitudinal rows of small pits are arranged on the wing cases and the latter, in addition, are covered with fine short hairs. The antennae are distinctly clubbed, the club being made up of two antennal segments. (In Common Furniture Beetle the antennae are not so distinctly clubbed and the club consists of three antennal segments.) *Lyctus* readily flies to light and in a room containing *Lyctus*-infested wood they may often be found around the windows at the time of emergence.

Life-cycle

Eggs. The eggs of *Lyctus* are long, cylindrical, rather maggot-like, with thread-like tails. They are translucent and whitish in colour, and are laid with great precision by the female, who inserts her long egg-laying tube into the open vessels or pores of the wood. These will either be exposed by the cutting or breaking of the wood or will have been exposed by the beetle herself by biting. The eggs are about 1 mm. in length but only about 0·15 mm. in width. Several eggs may be pushed into the same pore. Damage by *Lyctus* beetle is always restricted to the wide-pored hardwoods because of the physical requirements of egg-laying.

The larva. On hatching, the young larva first consumes some residual yolk in the egg which increases its girth to the extent that it is able to grip the side walls of the pore. After moulting, the body becomes strongly arched, the larva pierces the wall of the pore and thereafter tunnels in the woody tissue. At first the tunnel follows the grain but later it becomes seemingly haphazard and often cuts through the tunnels of other larvae or its own earlier tunnel. In the final stages of destruction the larvae tunnel mostly through faecal matter in order to find wood tissue which has not been chewed up. When fully grown the larva reaches a maximum length of 5 mm., the thorax is enlarged and the small legs consist of three segments only, the last of which is paddle-shaped. An easy means of distinguishing the *Lyctus* larva from that of *Anobium punctatum* is to examine the breathing pores (spiracles) situated along the side of the body. In the case of *Lyctus*, the spiracle on the eighth abdominal segment, the last spiracle, in fact, is large and easily detectable even without a lens, whilst in the case of *A. punctatum* all the spiracles are the same size and, even so, detectable only with difficulty.

The larva is not able to digest cellulose but subsists on the cell contents only.

Pupa. When the larva has finished feeding it bores towards the outer surface and immediately beneath the surface it constructs a rather large pupal chamber. The pupa is at first white then creamish but turns considerably darker a few days before metamorphosis.

Economic importance. Powder Post Beetles are pests of the sapwood of certain hardwoods only. The species of hardwood which are infested are those with wide pores or vessels large enough in diameter for the egg-laying tube of the female to be inserted in them for egg-laying. In addition, the sapwood must be rich in starch. Normally the female will not lay her eggs in the sapwood unless the required concentration of starch (thought to be about 3 per cent) is present. Oak and ash are two British timbers that come into this category, but a large number of tropical hardwoods are also susceptible to infestation by this species. This is a species which is of less importance at the present time than in the ten years or so immediately following the last war. This is almost certainly as a result of the large-scale effort to eradicate the pest from timber-yards where large stocks of oak were maintained. Because it is a pest of hardwoods it is normally confined in its attacks to furniture, hardwood floors and fittings.

The Wharf Borer, *Nacerdes melanura.* (See Fig. 31)

This insect, which is classified in the family OEDEMERIDAE, is native to the Great Lakes region of North America but the date of its introduction into Britain is not known.

Appearance. The adult beetle varies in length from about a quarter to half an inch in length. It gives the appearance of being rather a soft, flimsy insect of golden brown colour, although it may vary to a deeper reddish brown. The tips of the wing cases, however, are black, and this is

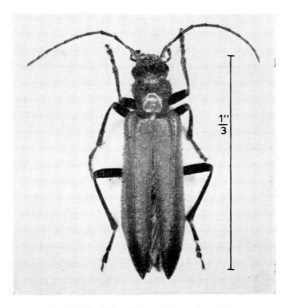

Fig. 31. The Wharf Borer, *Nacerdes melanura.*

the meaning of its specific name. The antennae are fairly long. The Wharf Borer may be confused with two other beetles, the Oak Longhorn, *Phymatodes testaceus*, found in timber-yards where its larvae feed on the superficial sapwood of unbarked logs, and a very common beetle of the countryside with many local names but which bears the scientific name *Rhagonycha fulva*. The Wharf Borer, however, may be separated from these two insects with ease, by the possession of three raised longitudinal ridges along the wing cases. This insect flies strongly.

Life-cycle

Larva. The inch-long greyish larva with its large yellow head cannot possibly be confused with any of the other species of wood-boring larvae. The thoracic legs are relatively large, and, in addition, situated on the sixth and seventh abdominal segments are a pair of stump-like false legs from which arise some spinules. There are patches of spinules also on the upper surface of the first five segments behind the head. The larvae do not normally construct well-defined tunnels but rather broad chambers which follow the grain of the timber. Frass is not produced in any quantity but a feature of Wharf Borer infested wood is the quantity of coarse wood scrapings in the larval chamber. All wood attacked by the larvae is wet, indeed it is often sodden and is always attacked by wood-rotting fungi such as *Merulius lacrymans*, causing dry rot, or by *Coniophora cerebella*, causing wet rot, The latter appears to predominate as the moisture content of the wood is considerably higher than that usual for dry rot fungus attack.

Economic importance. The typical habitat of this species is estuarine, where it attacks wood in piling, harbour works, driftwood, derelict boats and other timber buried or half-buried in sand or earth. It is common in most estuaries around the south coast but its headquarters appear to be the Thames estuary. In addition to the typical habitat, in the years following the war, it became a pest at the time of emergence in many London streets from the sheer numbers of the insect that invaded houses and commercial premises. This was because it was able to develop in wet exposed softwood timber on bomb-sites and even high up in the roof timbers of war-damaged buildings. With the passage of time the majority of these habitats have disappeared but it still remains in many London buildings where maintenance is poor, where hygiene standards are low, or where there are leaking lavatories, as the larvae appear to thrive in such conditions.

The life-cycle can take place through several generations in deeply buried woodwork.

The Bread Beetle, Biscuit Beetle or Drug Store Beetle, *Stegobium paniceum*. (See Plate IV)

This insect, a member of the family ANOBIIDAE, is not a wood-borer as are its two congeners, Common Furniture Beetle and Death Watch, which we have already considered.

Appearance. This is a small reddish to reddish-brown beetle only 2·0 to 3·5 mm. in length. The pronotum, which is rounded and is just as wide as the wing cases, completely masks the head which is inserted almost vertically beneath it. Very fine hairs are arranged in longitudinal rows on the wing cases. The terminal three segments of the antennae are larger than the basal segments (as in Furniture Beetle). It may be distinguished from the Furniture Beetle by the front margin of the pronotum being much more rounded.

Life-cycle. This is normally completed in about 7 months but increase in temperature diminishes this period considerably.

Eggs. About 100 eggs are laid singly in the foodstuff or in nearby crevices. This takes about 3 weeks and the eggs hatch in from 12 to 37 days.

Larva. The first-stage larva is extremely active and wanders about exploring its surroundings. It is small, measuring only 0·5 mm. in length and 0·125 mm. in breadth and can squeeze itself through very small crevices in packaged foodstuffs. At this stage it can survive starvation for 8 days. The entire larval stage lasts 4 to 5 months during which time the larva moults four times. When fully grown it measures 5 mm., is white in colour and is typically anobiid in shape as is the Furniture Beetle larva.

Pupa. The fully fed larva constructs a cocoon of food particles cemented together with a secretion from the mouth. The pupal stage lasts from 12 to 18 days when the adult finally bites its way out of the cocoon.

Economic importance. This is an important household pest which attacks stored food products and breeds in dried vegetable matter of many kinds. In domestic larders it feeds readily on flour, bread, farinaceous foods of diverse kinds, meat, soup powders, spices (especially red pepper), and has even been reported as infesting poisonous materials such as strychnine, belladonna and aconite. It is also a serious pest of books and manuscripts and has been known to bore in a straight line through a whole shelf of books. Tin foil and sheet lead may be perforated by this insect. Experiments on its nutrition show that it can complete its life-cycle in foods containing very small quantities of carbohydrates as it has symbiotic organisms resembling yeasts which produce vitamins of the 'B' group. The larva is therefore independent of external sources for this important accessory factor of nutrition.

The Mealworm Beetle, *Tenebrio molitor.* (See Plate III)

This beetle is classified in the family TENEBRIONIDAE, one of the largest families of the COLEOPTERA containing over 10,000 species. It contains a number of species of great economic importance throughout the world, including major pests of stored grain and grain products, but the above species is the only one thought to warrant inclusion in a book on insect pests likely to occur in the household.

Appearance. Varying from 12 to 16 mm. in length this beetle is dark, reddish-black in colour and shining. The wing cases bear longitudinal rows of small pits.

Note: A closely related species, *Tenebrio obscurus*, is less common than *T. molitor*, its wing cases are dull, not shining, but its biology is similar.

Life-cycle

The egg. Up to 576 eggs may be laid by one female either singly or in groups. They are bean-shaped and sticky and soon become covered with meal and debris.

The larva. The larvae (these are the 'mealworms') are long and cylindrical, the last two segments being conical. They are bright yellow, with each segment shading to yellowish-brown and have a shiny, waxy appearance. The legs are small but well developed. The number of moults varies widely from 9 to 20 and the larva reaches a length of up to 28 mm. (see Fig. 32).

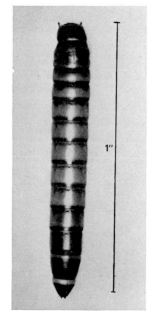

Fig. 32. The Mealworm, larva of *Tenebrio molitor*.

Pupa. When fully fed the larva passes through a prepupal stage when it lies on its side and assumes a curved posture. The resulting pupa is also curved and lies amongst the foodstuff and debris it has been infesting.

Length of life-cycle. At 18° to 20°C. the eggs take from 10 to 12 days to hatch and the larva lives 1 to 1½ years before pupating. The pupal stage lasts about 20 days. At 25°C. the larva lives from 6 to 8 months and the pupal stage 9 days. The total length of life-cycle varies from 280 to 630 days. The adult stage lasts 2 to 3 months.

Economic importance. This beetle is more likely to occur in dwellings such as old farmhouses, cottages, mills and other properties where grain and grain products have been stored and now remain as residues in underfloor spaces and other inaccessible situations. The Mealworms not only consume farinaceous material but will eat animal matter, such as dead insects if they come across it. They tend to occupy ill-ventilated, dark, damp situations but, in spite of this, at the emergence time in summer, the large black adult beetles may be seen making their way across the sitting-room floor usually when there are guests in the house!

The next three beetle pests to be described are members of the family PTINIDAE, and are fairly closely related to the ANOBIIDAE. Many of the 400 species of this family are cosmopolitan pests and fourteen species are known in Britain. As in the ANOBIIDAE the prothorax has the appearance of a cowl extending over the head so that only the antennae may be seen when the insect is viewed from the top.

Australian Spider Beetle, *Ptinus tectus.* (See Plate IV)

Although this species was not recorded in England until 1892 it is now one of the commonest and most widely distributed pests of stored products and miscellaneous food debris.

Appearance. The adult beetle varies from 3·5 to 4·0 mm. in length and is dull reddish-brown in colour. It is constricted at the junction of the prothorax and that part of the body covered by the wing cases to give a typical spider-like appearance. The wing cases are densely clothed with brown or golden-brown hair which hides the series of longitudinal rows of small pits which are only visible when the insect becomes rubbed and worn. The legs are long and ungainly, a feature which adds to the spider-like appearance. The adult beetle readily feigns death when disturbed and avoids the light. They drink freely and this prolongs life, resulting in more eggs being laid.

Life-cycle

Eggs. About 100 eggs are laid, either singly or in small groups. They are sticky when first laid and particles of food and debris adhere to them. They measure from 0·47 to 0·55 mm. in length and from 0.29 to 0·40 mm. in breadth and are opalescent in colour. Oviposition lasts about 3 to 4 weeks at normal temperature.

Larva. This is a whitish fleshy grub usually strongly curved which rolls up into a tight ball when disturbed. The legs are small but bear strong claws and the whole body is covered with fine hairs. When the larvae become fully fed they leave the foodstuff and wander about searching for a site for the cocoon. At this time the larva will bite its way through comparatively tough materials such as sacking, cellophane and cardboard. They will often hollow out chambers in adjacent woodwork. The spherical, thin-walled but tough cocoon is constructed from an oral secretion applied by the mouth parts.

Pupa. The extremely delicate pupa is white at first, but shortly before metamorphosis it turns golden brown. The adult remains within the cocoon for several days before biting its way out.

Length of life-cycle. This varies enormously according to temperature and relative humidity but usually takes about $3\frac{1}{2}$ months. At normal room temperature, egg-laying takes from 3 to 4 weeks; access to free water is important to the female at this stage. At temperatures between $68°$ and $77°$ F., the eggs hatch in 3 to 16 days but usually the period is from 5 to 7 days. The duration of the larval stage is upwards of 40 days. The pupal stage lasts from 20 to 30 days and after emergence the adults usually remain in the coccon for as long as three weeks. Under experimental conditions the length of life-cycle varied from $10\frac{1}{2}$ weeks in wholemeal flour at $27°$ C. to 36 weeks in casein at $20°$ C.

Economic importance. This insect is often found in stores, larders and warehouses, living more or less as a scavenger of miscellaneous debris including a wide range of dried materials of vegetable and animal origin. Whilst it thrives best on materials containing a high content of group B vitamins it can complete its development nevertheless in materials of relatively low nutritive content such as casein and pure starch. Apart from its scavenging habit it is commonly a pest of cereals, cereal products and spices and it often causes damage to containers of cardboard, sacking or wood at the cocoon-forming stage.

The Golden Spider Beetle, *Niptus hololeucus.* (See Plate IV)

This beetle originally came from the shores of the Black Sea but is now generally distributed in Europe.

Appearance. This spider-like beetle has the head concealed under the rounded prothorax and the abdomen is ovoid. The colour is golden-yellow with long silky hairs covering the wing cases which are fused down the centre line. The hind wings are absent. The antennae are relatively long. In length the beetle measures from 3.0 to 4·5 mm.

Life-cycle

The egg. This measures from 0·6 to 0·8 mm. in length and from 0·4 to 0·5 mm. in breadth. It is whitish opalescent and is sticky when first laid. The female may lay from 25 to 30 eggs during an egg-laying period of from 3 to 5 weeks.

Larva. There are said to be two moults only. In appearance it is similar to that of *Ptinus tectus.*

Pupa. The white pupa turns golden-brown shortly before emergence and the adult remains within the cocoon for some days before it bites its way out.

Length of life-cycle. From egg to adult usually takes from 6 to 7 months. The eggs hatch in from 11 to 20 days at temperatures between 64° and 68° F. and at this temperature the larval period lasts about 150 days. The pupal stage lasts from 18 to 26 days. The adult beetles are long-lived, 250 days having been recorded. Where there is an infestation the adult beetles are plentiful in June or July and again in October and November.

Economic importance. The Golden Spider Beetle is not an important pest of stored food but the larvae may damage cereals, cereal products, spices and drugs. They are most usually found amongst miscellaneous vegetable and animal debris in warehouses, poorly kept storerooms, cellars and old houses. The adult beetles sometimes occur in considerable numbers, giving rise to some degree of disquiet in the housewife, and they have been recorded as biting holes in textiles, garments, carpets and bedding. The adults shun the light but move actively in the dark. It is not such a widespread pest as is the Australian Spider Beetle.

The Hump Spider Beetle, *Gibbium psylloides*. (See Plate IV)

Appearance. This is a small beetle only 2 to 3 mm. in length with a curious rounded or humped shape. It is devoid of hairs and is of a bright shining reddish colour, giving it the appearance of a 'giant mite'. The under-surface of the abdomen is very small but the upper surface large and distended and a considerable air space exists under the wing cases. The under surface of the abdomen is covered with characteristic branched hairs. It is a much less active beetle than *Ptinus tectus*, its usual walking gait being very slow and rather cumbersome. When disturbed the adults feign death for a few seconds only then awkwardly scuttle away.

Life-cycle. Relatively few eggs are laid by the female. The immature stages are similar in appearance to those of *Ptinus tectus*. The cocoon is spherical and the larvae do not wander away from the foodstuff to pupate. It appears to thrive in rather drier conditions than other ptinids. In a series of experiments under controlled conditions, at 40 per cent relative humidity, 80 per cent of the eggs laid in wholemeal flour developed into adults. The total length of the life-cycle under various environmental conditions varied from 22 weeks to 42 weeks. The duration of adult life in these experiments was from 30 to 40 weeks but $18\frac{1}{2}$ months has been recorded (at 25° C.).

Economic importance. This species has long been known to infest old houses. Seeds, grain and grain products are the products most commonly infested but in addition it is found in various types of vegetable debris. Woollen materials and paper have been damaged by this insect and it shares with other ptinids the habits of being able to thrive on drugs including opium. Tallow has also been infested.

The three beetles whose descriptions follow, belong to the family DERMESTIDAE. These are the Hide Beetles and Carpet Beetles and the family name literally means 'skin eater'. Altogether about 700 species are known and although most are rather small, measuring only from 2 to 4 mm., a few reach 12 mm. Most of them are characterized by the body being covered with distinctive patterns of hairs or scales. The prothorax bears a pair of grooves into which the antennae may be retracted.

The Larder or Bacon Beetle, *Dermestes lardarius*

Appearance. This is one of the larger species of DERMESTIDAE measuring from 5·5 to 12 mm. in length. The beetle is oval in shape. The front half of each wing case is pale in colour, with a transverse band of spots or marks across the centre of it. The prothorax is dark in colour with a number of pale spots mostly situated around the margin. The antennae are strongly clubbed, the club consisting of three segments.

Note. The closely related species *Dermestes maculatus* is less commonly found than *D. lardarius* but its biology is similar. It lacks the pale areas in the front half of the wing cases and its underside is silvery white.

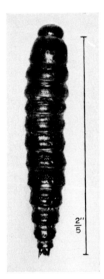

Fig. 33. Larva of Larder Beetle, *Dermestes lardarius*.

Life-cycle

The egg. It is necessary for the female beetle to eat before she lays her eggs; she requires the same type of food as that consumed by the larvae. The eggs are 2 mm. in length and are laid in crevices amongst the food-stuffs such as hides and other dry animal matter. Egg-laying continues for 2 or 3 months and the total number of eggs laid varies from 200 to 800.

Larva. On hatching, the larva is white but within a few hours assumes a darker coloration. The larva is covered with strong bristle-like hairs of different sizes, the shorter ones being borne in tufts. They feed continuously in the dark on fairly dry animal matter and are active and fairly agile, but in the light, if disturbed, they become immobile, feigning death. When an abundant supply of foodstuff is present the faecal pellets are excreted in a bead-like chain. The larvae moult 5 or 6 times but under some conditions as many as 12 moults have been observed. The fully grown larva measures from 10 to 15 mm. (see Fig. 33).

Pupa. When the larva is mature it wanders away from the foodstuff it has been consuming to seek a pupation site and it is at this time that it will burrow into such substances as wood before assuming the pupal state. Sometimes the tunnels are short, just long enough for the larva to get inside the wood, but at other times the tunnels extend for several inches and have been reported as long as 12 inches. When the final larval skin is cast it acts as a plug protecting the naked pupa from predaceous insects. If, however, the larva for some reason is unable to bore a tunnel the larval skin remains attached to the pupa.

Length of life-cycle. At 17° C. the eggs hatch in 9 days but at high temperatures, 25° to 28° C., this is reduced to 2½ days. The pupal stage usually lasts 8 to 15 days only, and at 18° to 25° C. the whole life-cycle takes place in 2 to 3 months. The adult beetles are fairly long-lived, it being quite usual for them to live for over 3 months and they often hibernate as adults in unheated premises.

Economic importance. The Larder Beetle is a common pest of many types of industrial and commercial premises where dry animal protein, in numerous forms, is processed or stored. Tanyards, hide and skin warehouses, and premises where bones and pet foods are processed are the usual situations where this pest may attain major importance. In household larders, this species infests cheese, bacon and ham, but as there is less home-curing and cheese-making these days, the insect is not so prevalent as in former times.

In addition to the above, however, the Larder Beetle sometimes causes damage to museum specimens, such as stuffed animals, and it occurs also in beehives where dead bees and wax are eaten. Specimens found in dwellings often have been feeding on the bodies of dead mice under floor-boards or dead birds in the chimney or roof void.

The Varied Carpet Beetle, *Anthrenus verbasci*. (See Fig. 35)

This species is taken as an example, being perhaps the most common species of *Anthrenus* found on carpets in dwellings in the south of England. In addition, other species may sometimes be present in homes, and a note about one of the species is given below.

Appearance. Anthrenus beetles are fairly small, measuring only 1·5 to 4 mm. in length. Although oval in shape, they are much rounder than other dermestid beetles found in households. The body is strongly convex, rather like the Ladybird Beetles (COCCINELLIDAE). *Anthrenus* beetles are characterized by the pattern of yellow, black and whitish dense scales covering the pronotum and elytra.

Life-cycle

The egg. Between 20 and 100 eggs are laid by the female during spring and early summer on furs, woollens and any dried materials of animal origin. The eggs are lightly cemented to the foodstuff sufficiently strongly that they are not dislodged by shaking. The female begins laying four days or so after fertilization and continues for one to two weeks.

Fig. 34. Larva of Varied Carpet Beetle,
Anthrenus verbasci.

The larva. This is hairy and brown with a bunch of special golden hairs on each side of the rear abdominal segments. These hairs are shaped like arrows, the details of the heads of which are used for identifying the different species. If a larva is disturbed it rolls up and in so doing fans out these hairs, giving the larva the appearance of a small golden ball. The larva usually moults 6 or 8 times but under adverse conditions, such as in semi-starvation, the number of moults may be as many as 30. If a larva has been feeding well, it can resist starvation to a remarkable degree. In the case of the Common Carpet Beetle, a ten-month starvation period has been recorded. *Anthrenus* larvae avoid the light and they often pupate inside their food material, this being commonly the case if a dead insect is being consumed. The larvae reach a length of 4 to 5 mm. (see Fig. 34).

Pupa. The last larval skin is not shed but remains as a complete cover to the pupa. The adult too remains within the last larval skin before emergence for a period varying from 4 days or so to as long as a month.

Length of life-cycle. The eggs hatch in from 10 days at 29·4°C. to 35 days at 18·3°C. but there appears to be no experimental data on the length of larval life under controlled conditions, although this would seem to depend very much on the nutritional value of the foodstuff being consumed. Larvae are hardly able to complete their development on clean wool or feathers, but if soiled with excrement or other materials of high protein content, development proceeds normally. At room temperature a batch of larvae took from 222 to 323 days to complete their development, with the exception of two eventual females that took 604 and 630 days. Out of doors the winter is passed in the larval stage. The pupal stage takes from 7 days at 29·4°C. to 19 days at 18·3°C. The duration of the adult life varies

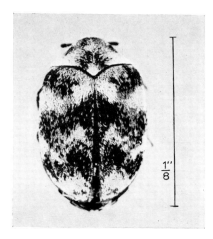

Fig. 35. Varied Carpet Beetle, *Anthrenus verbasci.*

from 7 to 41 days. In temperate climates there is usually one generation a year but there could be nearly two as in Germany, where a 7 month and a 14 month life-cycle has been observed. The adults appear in April, May and June and their resulting larvae hibernate during the following winter, pupating during the latter part of February and March. A few larvae, however, do not overwinter but produce adults in September.

Economic importance. This insect has been recorded from a host of different materials and although it is considered to be of greatest importance as attacking woollen materials, yet it has often been reported as infesting grain products, seeds of various sorts, cacao and other products of vegetable origin. Most of the older records concern the destruction of insect collections, but from the 1930s onwards it has become of increasing importance in its attacks on woollen carpets and garments. The manner of the insect's distribution is of interest and importance. On emergence, the adult beetles seek the light and fly to light-coloured flowers where they feed on nectar and pollen. After mating, the females enter houses and lay their eggs in birds' nests in roof voids and in other suitable places. The larvae feed on feathers and wool soiled with excrement, dead fledglings, etc. From this site they wander downwards, probably aware of the heat gradient, until they reach airing cupboards, clothes cupboards or wardrobes. They continue feeding in warm dry conditions which are found in such situations and may wander further to carpets.

Note: In addition to the species given above, *Anthrenus fuscus* is quite a common insect in buildings; indeed, it is sometimes thought to be second to *A. verbasci* in numbers. However, it is not a wool feeder but is a common associate of spiders' webs in corners of rooms and windows where it feeds on the remains of insects discarded by the spiders. *A. fuscus* may be identified from all other species in this genus by the antennae, which have only 5 segments.

The Fur Beetle, *Attagenus pellio.* (See Plate III)

The Black Carpet Beetle, *Attagenus piceus*

These two closely related species are described together in the following account.

Appearance. These beetles are intermediate in size between *Dermestes* and *Anthrenus*, being 3·6 to 5·7 mm. in length and in breadth 1·8 to 3·0 mm. In colour, both species are dark reddish-brown to black, the basal segments of the antennae and the legs being of a rather pale brownish colour. *A. pellio* is separated from *A. piceus* by the occurrence of small patches of white or yellowish hairs, the most striking of which occur in the centre of each wing case. Three smaller patches are located along the hind margin of the pronotum. The antennae have a three-segmented club. In the male, the last antennal segment is much enlarged, being about as long as the remainder of the antenna, but in the case of the female the terminal segment is only about as long as the combined length of the two adjacent segments.

Life-cycle

The egg. After mating has taken place on flowers out of doors, the female flies into dwellings and lays her 50 to 100 eggs on materials suitable for larval food, such as woollen carpets, birds' nests, and any other dried substance of animal origin.

The larva. The larvae are hairy and are characterized by the possession of a tuft of long hairs arising from the terminal segment of the abdomen. The larva has a banded appearance and the cast skins show this character to much greater degree, these cast skins often being a feature of an infestation. The larvae avoid the light and when disturbed they often remain immobile for a time in a slightly curved posture. The number of moults varies

PLATE III opposite: 1. Common Furniture Beetle,   2. Powder Post Beetle,
3. Fur Beetle, 4. Mealworm Beetle.

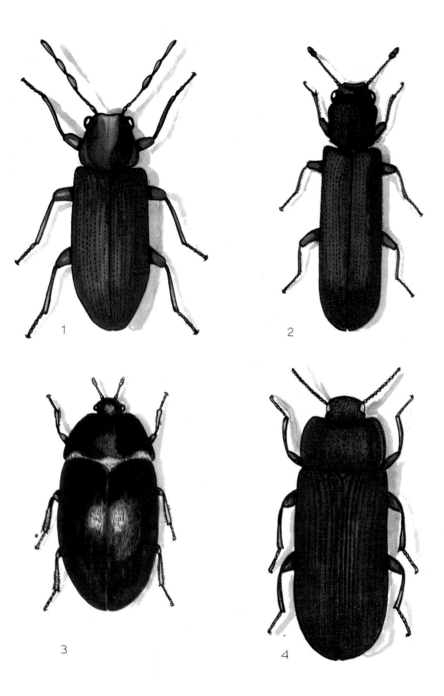

1

2

3

4

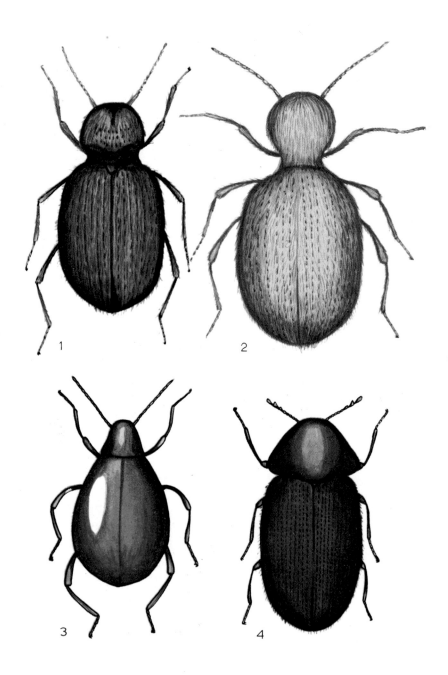

according to temperature and availability and type of foodstuff, but 6 to 20 is normal (see Fig. 36).

The pupa. The pupa is never visible, as pupation occurs within the last larval skin. When the adult stage has been assumed the beetle remains within the larval skin for a period of 3 to 20 days before it emerges to seek the light and to feed on the pollen and nectar of flowers.

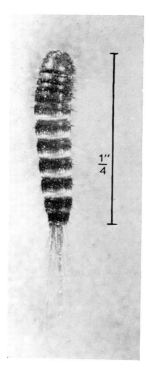

Fig. 36. Larva of the Fur Beetle, *Attagenus pellio.*

Length of life-cycle. The eggs hatch in from 22 days at 18°C. to 6 days at 30°C. The length of the larval stage depends mainly on foodstuffs, but takes 65 to 184 days at temperatures between 25 and 30°C. The pupal stage lasts from 18 days at 18°C. to $5\frac{1}{2}$ days at 30°C. In general, under normal household conditions, an annual life-cycle takes place, but periods of 6 months to 3 years are not unusual. The adult beetle does not require to feed on the larval foodstuff before egg-laying commences.

Economic importance. In Britain *A. pellio* is much the commoner of the two species but in America and Asia it is *A. piceus* which is the dominant species of the genus. There is reason to believe that *A. pellio* has increased

PLATE IV opposite: 1. Australian Spider Beetle, 2. Golden Spider Beetle, 3. Hump Spider Beetle, 4. Bread Beetle.

in importance as a pest in Britain since the war. It is a common inhabitant of birds' nests out of doors and from such sites the larvae probably invade domestic premises. Most commonly it is found in our homes infesting carpets, stored woollen garments, skins and furs, but in addition it has been recorded as infesting a large number of materials from those of high protein content such as museum specimens of insects, bones, smoked fish and meat, dried yolk of eggs, casein and silk in various forms, to products of high carbohydrate content such as grain, cereal products, flour, semolina, maize meal, rye bran, sugar and similar materials. It is not known to what extent in these cases the *A. pellio* larvae were feeding on dead insect remains of previous infestations. The larvae of this beetle have been shown to be capable of carrying the bacilli of *Anthrax* both on their body and in their faeces.

Ladybird Beetles, COCCINELLIDAE. (See Fig. 37)

The well-known Ladybird Beetles are often found indoors. Usually this is only for hibernation during the winter months. The following brief account gives some general information concerning a few of the 45 British species.

Appearance. Ladybird Beetles are roundish-oval in shape, strongly convex above and flat beneath. The species that concern us are shiny and almost always show conspicuous markings in black, yellow, red and white. These are the so-called 'warning' colours which are associated with insects that are inedible or unpalatable to insectivorous animals, such as some species

Fig. 37. A Ladybird Beetle, *Adalia bipunctata.*

$\frac{1''}{5}$

of birds and mammals. The colour patterns of the common species are very variable. *Adalia bipunctata* measures 3 to 4 mm. in length, has a black spot on each red wing cover and is exceedingly common. *Adalia decempunctata* is also very common. *Coccinella septempunctata* has bright red wing covers with three black spots on each and a single shared black spot at the base.

Life-cycle

The egg. These are laid in batches of from 3 to 50 on the under-side of leaves, usually where there is an abundance of aphids. They are orange-yellow in colour and are placed on the leaf with their long axes perpendicular to the leaf. In the case of *A. bipunctata* as many as 418 eggs have been laid by one female but between 100 and 200 appears to be more usual.

Larva. The bluish-grey larva variously patterned with brighter colours consumes several hundred aphids during its short larval life. It does not appear to be very active but its prey are not agile enough to evade it.

Pupa. Pupation takes place on a leaf and the larval skin remains attached to the pupa.

Length of life-cycle. The eggs hatch in 5 to 11 days; the larval life lasts 3 weeks and the pupal life one week. The total length of life-cycle varies according to conditions from 27 to 49 days.

Economic importance. By preying on plant lice (aphids) the Ladybird (in both the adult and the larval stage) proves to be an important beneficial insect in the garden. Their occurrence in buildings in winter (and sometimes in summer) is on account of their habit of hibernating in situations where climatic conditions are somewhat less severe than those encountered outdoors. Ladybirds, when hibernating, also display the habit of congregating, sometimes in large numbers, and this is thought to be associated with their warning coloration, more of such insects obviously having a much greater visual effect on marauding insectivorous animals than would single individuals.

Ground Beetles, CARABIDAE

This large family is belived to be the most primitive of beetles and is usually amongst the first families considered in any work on the COLEOPTERA. Throughout the world there are something like 25,000 species and 344 of these are found in Britain, although only a few of the very common species occurring in our gardens and entering our houses concern us in this present work. Most commonly it is the species *Harpalus rufipes* which is implicated and the following account deals mainly with this species.

Appearance. The general distinguishing features of the family CARABIDAE are as follows:

They are always very active beetles with long legs and usually they are fairly large, being half an inch or more in length. In colour they may be blackish and there is often a strong metallic lustre. The antennae consisting of 11 segments are never clubbed. There are always five tarsal segments. The body is usually somewhat flattened. Viewing the beetle from underneath the first abdominal segment is completely divided by the hind coxae (the first or basal segment of the legs) and there are 6 visible abdominal segments. *Harpalus rufipes*, which measures 14 to 16 mm. in length, is black with the antennae, mouth parts and legs of a reddish-brown colour. The pronotum is divided by a fine longitudinal depression; the wing cases bear a number of longitudinal ridges, and are clothed with long reddish hairs (see Fig. 38).

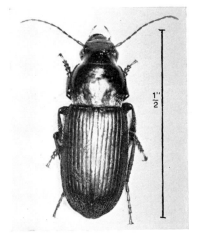

Fig. 38. The Strawberry Seed Beetle, *Harpalus rufipes*.

Life-cycle. No detailed observations appear to have been made on the life-cycle of *Harpalus rufipes*, but it is probably an annual one and the adults probably live for a considerable period.

Economic importance. This species often occurs in the ground-floor rooms of houses during the summer months, when they wander into the house from the garden. They are adept at forcing their way into narrow cracks under stones and it is likely that they are able to squeeze their flat bodies under the kitchen door so that they can be looked upon merely as fortuitous wanderers from the garden. Out of doors both the larvae and the adults are voracious predators, feeding on moth caterpillars and slugs and snails, thus performing a beneficial role. On the other hand, they are reported as sometimes feeding on vegetable matter such as strawberries and causing great damage.

A number of instances have been reported where, instead of one or two individuals of *Harpalus rufipes* entering houses, the numbers have been of plague proportions. In one recorded instance between 500 and 600 beetles entered one house every night. The reasons for infestation on such a scale are not known. It is sometimes found in warehouses and granaries.

The Plaster Beetles. (See Figs. 39, 40 and 41)

The following six beetle species found in houses are known as 'Plaster' or 'Fungus' beetles. This is because they are usually present in a house shortly after its erection when the plastering is new and still very damp. In such conditions surface-growing moulds and mildews occur on plaster, paper and wood and it is on these fungi that the larvae and the adult plaster beetles subsist.

Two families of beetles are referred to as Plaster Beetles and the commonest species likely to be found in houses are as follows:

CRYPTOPHAGIDAE
Cryptophagus acutangulus
Cryptophagus cellaris
Cryptophagus distinguendus

LATHRIDIIDAE
Lathridius (Coninomus) nodifer
Lathridius bergrothi
Enicmus minutus

$\dfrac{1''}{12}$

Fig. 39. The Plaster Beetle,
Lathridius (Coninomus) nodifer.

There are 80 species of CRYPTOPHAGIDAE found in Britain and of these *Cryptophagus cellaris* is probably the most widely distributed, but it is found in mills, warehouses and large damp cellars more often than in dwellings. *C. acutangulus*, however, is most common in the latter type of premises. In the LATHRIDIIDAE there are 48 British species of which the three species noted above most commonly occur in households.

What is known concerning the detailed biology of the various species of Plaster Beetles shows no significant differences so that they are dealt with in this account as a group.

Fig. 40. The Plaster Beetle,
Lathridius bergrothi.

Appearance. All Plaster Beetles are small, mostly within the length of 1·0 to 2·5 mm. In both families the antennae are clubbed; the club consisting of three segments. Those species in the CRYPTOPHAGIDAE are characterized by the shape of the pronotum which is thickened at the front and bears a tooth at the centre of each side. The greatest width of the pronotum is approximately equal to the width of the wing cases. In the LATHRIDIIDAE,

Fig. 41. The Plaster Beetle,
Enicmus minutus.

on the other hand, the width of the pronotum is often much less than the width of the wing cases, and a feature common to the three species being considered in this account, is the strong longitudinal ridging of the wing cases or rows of deep pits. In the species *Lathridius nodifer* the ridging extends to the pronotum. Plaster Beetles are dark in colour, varying from reddish-brown to black.

Life-cycle

The egg. The egg of *Enicmus minutus* is laid singly and is 0·47 mm. in length and 0·18 mm. in width. It is oblong with one side slightly concave. In colour the egg is shiny whitish opalescent.

The larva. It grows to a length of 2·2 mm. and each thoracic and abdominal segment bears a number of backward-curling setae which in the species *Lathridius* (*Coninomus*) *nodifer* are exceptionally long. When about to pupate the larva of *Enicmus minutus* secretes a sticky substance from the anus which cements it to the substrate.

The pupa. The length of the pupa of *Enicmus minutus* is 1·53 mm. It is whitish in colour and after a few days the eyes are reddish. When viewed from above the head is concealed by the pronotum.

Length of life-cycle. When *Enicmus minutus* was reared on mouldy bread at a mean temperature of 62° to 65° F. the eggs hatched in 5 or 6 days. Each of the first two instars lasted 4 to 5 days. The third instar larvae fed for 3 or 4 days and then wandered around for 2 or 3 days before pupating. The pupal period was found to be 6 to 7 days but periods of 14 and 15 days have been reported, the differences are almost certainly due to differences in rearing temperature. The complete life-cycle from egg-laying to adult emergence varied from 24 to 30 days.

Economic importance. Plaster Beetles and their larvae feed exclusively on the hyphae and spores of moulds, mildews and other fungi. They can, therefore, only exist under the same conditions of dampness as required for fungal growth. As a result they are found in damp cellars, granaries and warehouses, as well as in new or newly converted houses, where moulds may have developed on walls and unpainted woodwork, due to incomplete drying out of plaster and the associated high humidity of the air. Joinery with a high moisture content will often support surface-growing fungi on which Plaster Beetles and their larvae will feed. Under such conditions, if an infestation occurs, it will not continue for longer than three or four months if the house is dried out with heat and good ventilation. Although Plaster Beetles occur in warehouses, they cannot be considered important food pests although they are sometimes found to be contaminating foodstuffs with their faeces if the foodstuff is slightly damp, and thus encouraging mould growth. It is thought that Plaster Beetles may be responsible for transmitting moulds from one commodity to another. At least one species, *Cryptophagus acutangulus*, is known to thrive on the Dry Rot fungus *Merulius lacrymans*. The natural habitat of these insects is amongst mouldy vegetable debris, under the bark of dead and decaying trees, and in the nests of ants, social wasps and birds. The adult beetles are also found in flowers.

The Short-Nosed Weevils, *Otiorrhynchus* species

Two members of the Weevil family, the CURCULIONIDAE, have already been described in this chapter, these were the Wood-boring Weevils, *Euophryum confine* and *Pentarthrum huttoni*. Brief mention must be made, however, of certain species of Weevils belonging to a group in which the rostrum or snout is short and stumpy.

Like all Weevils they are vegetarians, the legless larvae feeding on the roots of low-growing plants. Sometimes certain species, such as *Otiorrhynchus sulcatus*, can be present in such large numbers that it can be looked upon as a serious garden pest as it may damage such plants as strawberries and greenhouse plants.

Fig. 42. The Garden Weevil, *Otiorrhynchus rugostriatus*.

The adults often wander into dwellings, especially in autumn, to seek shelter for the winter. They do no damage, and are merely an annoyance to the householder who may confuse them with woodworm beetles. See the Garden Weevil, *Otiorrhynchus rugostriatus*, in Fig. 42.

9

WASPS AND ANTS

Hymenoptera

The four household insect pests which follow are classified in the order
HYMENOPTERA. This is a large order made up of about 60,000 species
distributed throughout the world. Members of the order are characterized
by the possession of two pairs of wings, the front pair larger than the hind
pair. They are fastened together by a row of small hooks along part of the
front edge of the hind wings which lock with a corresponding curled-over
length of the hinder edge of the front wings. The mouth parts are adapted
for biting and sometimes for sucking or lapping-up liquids. A large number
of hymenopterous insects show the 'wasp waist', a constriction occurring
at the second abdominal segment, the first segment being fused to the
thorax. The female possesses an ovipositor which may be modified for
sawing, piercing or stinging. The larva is almost always legless, with a
well-developed head. A large number of insects in this group are beneficial
to man and outstanding in this respect is the Honey-Bee which, besides
producing honey, is of immense importance as a pollinator of flowers.
In addition to this insect a large number of species, known as ichneumon
flies, and some related groups are of extreme importance as parasites of
harmful insects which they keep in check.

The order HYMENOPTERA is also of great interest on account of the
social communities which exist in a number of species more particularly
the Honey Bee, the 'social' wasps and ants.

The Wasp, *Paravespula vulgaris* and *Paravespula germanica*

Wasps, with their characteristic yellow-and-black markings, are familiar
insects to everyone, being common during late summer and autumn, until
the first cold weather brings their activity to an end (see Figs. 43 and 44).

Although the name 'wasp' includes all our six native species (which to
the householder would probably be indistinguishable from one another),
those that most commonly enter houses belong to the two species whose
scientific names are given above. In the account which follows both common species are included except when differences are discussed.

Appearance. It has been said that the average man considers that he can distinguish a bee from a wasp, and either from a fly. But he fails to realise that bees are legion, and some insects that he supposes to be bees are only flies; some of his wasps are also flies and others bees! The errors that the average man makes are due to reliance on colour pattern as the feature of identification and man is not the only animal that makes this error. Indeed this error has had a profound effect on the colour pattern of other insects and is associated with the wasp's capacity to inflict a painful sting.

Insects, like other animals, vary slightly in their shape and coloration, and during the course of evolution those producing varieties which caused them to be mistaken for wasps, however momentarily, by insect-eating birds and other animals, had a greater chance of survival. It has come about

Fig. 43. Queen Common Wasp, *Paravespula vulgaris*.

that many insects bear the black-and-yellow transverse bands of the wasp, such as many species of flies of a number of different families, moths and even several species of beetles.

In spite of what is written above the wasp is such a well-known insect that it is not intended to give a detailed description. The reader, should, however, recognize the essential features, the four wings locking together, the large head with its long axis, and the mouth parts directed vertically downwards. The queen is about 20 mm. in length, the males about 15 mm., and the workers 10 to 15 mm. in length. The males in each species possess longer antennae than the queens and workers.

Life-cycle. The young queens emerge from the nest in autumn and, after mating, select hibernation sites in protected situations, such as garden sheds and under bark. They normally cling with their jaws to material such as sacking or curtains. It is not until late in the following spring that hibernation comes to an end and the surviving queens select nest sites. The two common species nest in the ground in banks, or sometimes amongst roof rafters or in sheds. The queen builds her nest of wood which she has scraped from a fence post, and after it has been mixed with saliva she spreads it out with her jaws and tongue to make a slightly undulating fragile wafer-like paper.

Fig. 44. Queen German Wasp, *Paravespula germanica.*

The nest consists of an outer covering of several layers of paper, and a number of combs each consisting of many six-sided cells. A single egg is laid in each cell by the queen. Seven to 10 days later, the larvae hatch and are fed on dead insects by the queen. When fully fed, the larva seals its cell with a silk-like membrane and then pupates. When the final transformation takes place the wasp, a sterile worker, bites its way out of the cell and helps in all the activities of the colony except egg-laying, which only the queen is capable of carrying out. From laying the egg to emergence of the adult takes from 3 to 6 weeks. The workers excavate the nest cavity, build more combs, feed the larvae with insects and later in the year construct the large cells for queen-rearing (see Fig. 45).

On average each cell in the comb is used twice and in a nest of seven combs it is estimated that between 25,000 and 30,000 wasps may be reared during the season.

Towards the end of the summer the original queen lays a number of eggs which produce male wasps only and these mate with the new queens.

At the onset of the cold weather during the autumn all the wasps die, with the exception of the new queens which fly away seeking hibernating sites.

Economic importance. Wasps cause considerable nuisance as they are attracted to fruit, jam and similar sweet substances. In years of great abundance they cause much economic loss in premises where confectionery, jam and preserves are made, due to the interference with production. Work is often held up by invasions of wasps during the summer months. It is not generally known that the painful stings of wasps cause several deaths each year.

The sting. The sting of the wasp is a relatively simple mechanism (see Fig. 46). It is mainly contained in a cavity at the tip of the abdomen which is protected by the last plates of the abdomen, both dorsal and ventral, the actual slit being crescentric in shape. The point of the sting may often be observed protruding from the slit. If the sting is distended by pressing the abdomen (make sure the wasp is dead!) two 'sting palps' may be seen. On closer examination the sting is seen to consist of three parts. There is a

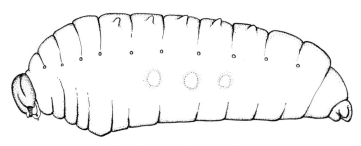

Fig. 45. Grub of Common Wasp.

sting sheath with a bulb at its base which is hollow but open on the under-surface. The opening is closed by two long stylets, the tips of which are sharp and barbed and project beyond the sting sheath. The base of the sting sheath, which is bulb-like, is produced into two curved arms and the inner parts of the stylets follow the same curves. The inner parts of the stylets articulate with the abdominal plates. Abdominal muscles cause the plates to drive the sting into the flesh of the victim. Two long glands secrete the venom which is stored in the poison sac. When the sting is brought into use the venom is forced from the sac into an enlargement at the inner end of the sting sheath and is then forced along the channel into the wound.

The venom has two main constituents, histamine and apitoxin. The old-fashioned remedy for the relief of wasp stings was to use an alkali such as washing-soda. This has little effect on the poisons injected by the wasp, and the modern, more effective, treatment is to liberally apply an antihistamine cream to the site of the sting and to take antihistamine tablets by mouth.

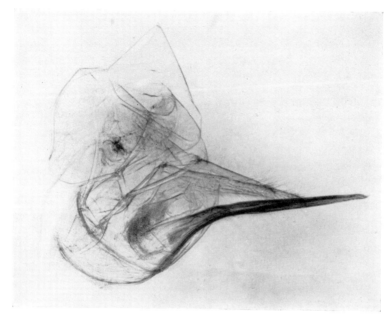

Fig. 46. Sting of Wasp.

ANTS, FORMICIDAE

Ants constitute a single family in the order HYMENOPTERA known as the
FORMICIDAE. They are characterized by the main divisions of the body
being distinctly separated; the abdomen consists of a very narrow 'waist'
composed of one or two segments called the *pedicel*, and a globular part
known as the *gaster*. The antennae are strongly elbowed. The most remarkable feature of the ants, however, is the social organizations in which
they live and the various forms assumed by the adult insects according to
the tasks which they perform in the community and for which they have
been specially reared.

What are known commercially as 'ants' eggs', used for feeding aquarium
fishes, are not the eggs but the pupae in their paper-like cocoons.

Pharaoh's Ant, *Monomorium pharaonis.* (See Fig. 47)

This species is not native to Britain having been imported from the tropics
over a hundred years ago. It has now adapted itself to an indoor environment.

Appearance. This is a very small species, the workers measuring only 2·0
mm. in length. The queens, that is the females, measure 3·6 mm. and the
males 3·0 mm. They are light yellow in colour and only the sexually
mature individuals of both sexes bear wings.

Life-cycle. Pharaoh's Ant develops in colonies within nests, but unlike many other ants, there are usually many queens. The various colonies live amicably together and form large aggregate nests. This species builds new colonies which, apparently, are formed by workers and adults evacuating the old site and taking eggs and larvae with them. This mode of formation of a new colony is quite exceptional amongst the ants and it is thought that, in this species, adults alone cannot build up a new colony. Such migrations may occur at any time of the year when the old nest becomes overcrowded.

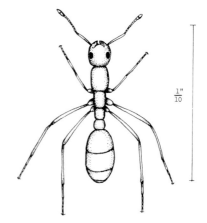

Fig. 47. Pharaoh's Ant
Monomorium pharaonis.

$\frac{1}{10}$"

They are relatively unaffected by seasons so that sexual forms are usually produced and found throughout the year.

Up to 300 eggs are laid by the young queen, in batches of 10 to 12 for the first few days, and later in batches of 4 to 7. The eggs take approximately $7\frac{1}{2}$ days to hatch into legless larvae which the queen feeds by regurgitating food from her mouth. She herself has taken no food since she mated.

These first larvae are fully grown in 18 days. Pupation usually takes 9 days and the average time for development of a worker is about 38 days, but the sexual forms take 4 or more days longer.

The workers are females in which the sexual organs have failed to develop and it is the workers that are responsible for the provision of food and the nourishment of the females and larvae. In addition to this the workers attend to the sanitation of the nest. From time to time fertile females and males are produced which develop from large, well-fed larvae.

Mating usually takes place in the wall spaces and crevices of infested buildings and the nuptial flights of winged sexuals of our native species, which are a common sight in summer, are never observed even though the sexual forms are winged.

Economic importance. Pharaoh's Ant is attracted to situations where there is a high temperature and a relatively high humidity. It frequently infests buildings in which food is stored and handled and is found in kitchens, canteens, bakehouses, hotels and hospitals, and it frequently spreads from such situations to bedrooms. All kinds of human food are attacked, especially jam, sugar and honey, and in addition meat, cheese and fats are often infested. Dead cockroaches, dead mice and mouse droppings are often devoured. Trails to the food supply and back to the nest usually follow well-defined pathways. The nests are often in inaccessible parts of houses, such as under floors, within walls, behind stoves or in the vicinity of hot-water pipes and this makes their detection and eradication difficult.

In hospitals, Pharaoh's Ant is known to enter beds in considerable numbers; they are known to bite young infants and it is thought that the mechanical transmission of disease germs is possible due to their habit of visiting damp situations such as drains, excreta, wet dressings and sputum.

Black Garden Ant, *Lasius (Acanthomyops) niger.* (See Fig. 48)

This species of ant is indigenous to Britain and is widely distributed. As well as being found in many natural situations it is common in gardens around houses and enters dwellings when foraging for food. Considerable annoyance is caused by such intrusions.

Appearance. As its name implies, this is a black ant although more accurately it is of a blackish-brown hue and the base of the antennae, the jaws, the feet and the base of the leg-joint are yellowish. In length they vary from 3 to 5 mm., there being two distinct sizes of worker, the 'major' and 'minor'. The male may be differentiated from the female by its posses-

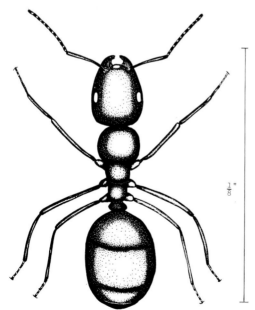

Fig. 48. Garden Ant, *Lasius niger.*

sion of a smaller head, but longer antennae. Around buildings, the nest openings may easily be distinguished by small piles of fine earth brought up from under flagstones.

Life-cycle. The swarming flight of the newly emerged males and females is a common sight on a hot sunny afternoon in July or August. Certain specific climatic conditions are obviously essential as the swarming of the colonies takes place simultaneously over a wide area. Mating takes place in the air, and within a few days the male dies. The female cuts off her wings and either returns to the original colony or she finds a suitable situation by digging a tunnel under a stone, where she will remain until the following spring before she commences to lay eggs. They hatch in from 22 to 28 days and the young queen rests during this period. When the larvae hatch she feeds them with a salivary substance from her own mouth during the whole of this stage, which lasts 16 to 23 days. New workers emerge from the pupae and these then nurse, tend and feed the larvae hatching from new batches of eggs (laid by the queen) and the queen herself. The workers leave the nest and forage for dead insects, sweet materials such as nectar from flowers and honeydew, a secretion of aphids. The Black Garden Ant is one of the species which tend and 'herd' aphids, milking them of their honeydew from time to time. This food is fed to the larvae by regurgitation in a liquid condition.

Economic importance. It is the foraging habit of the workers which brings them into the home, and when a rich source of food such as sugar, syrup or similar sweet food is found, the information soon gets back to a host of workers who thereafter cluster onto it in large numbers and form a steady stream back to the nest. Such food is often rejected by the housewife although this species is not known to transmit disease. Insects in the larder are always a cause of annoyance and anxiety and the Black Garden Ant, finding its way through minute cracks in brickwork of walls, is a common source of worry.

10

FLIES AND GNATS

Cluster Fly—Window Gnat—House Fly—Seaweed Fly—Fruit Fly—Mosquitoes and
other two-winged flies

Diptera

THE TRUE OR TWO-WINGED FLIES, DIPTERA

DIPTERA literally means 'two-winged' and, indeed, only the front pair of
wings are functional and they are clear and membraneous. The hind wings
are represented by a pair of small knob-like organs called *halteres* or
balancers. The adult 'fly' does not possess mandibles but the mouth parts
are modified into a proboscis for sucking or for piercing and sucking. The
larva is legless and the head is often reduced or indistinguishable and
retracted into the thoracic segments.

The two-winged flies constitute a large order of insects and about 50,000
different species are known throughout the world, about 3000 of which are
found in Britain. This group forms one of the most highly specialized of
insect orders and many species are of the utmost significance in regard to
human welfare. The pathogenic organisms of such diseases as malaria,
sleeping sickness, onchocerciasis, elephantiasis and yellow fever are carried
from man to man by blood-sucking dipterous flies. Many other diseases
are transmitted mechanically by flies due to the habit exhibited by many
species of sucking liquid from excreta and other decaying organic matter
and then settling on human food.

The Cluster Fly, *Pollenia rudis*. (See Fig. 49)

This species is classified in the family CALLIPHORIDAE.

Appearance. This is a largish fly measuring up to one-third of an inch in
length. The thorax is dark greyish-olive and clothed with densely matted
golden hairs, whilst the abdomen has shifting chequered reflections with a
dark middle line. When closed, the wings are folded on top of each other
over the abdomen, scissor-like, and not diverging at the tips.

Life-cycle. The larva of this species lives as a parasite of a certain species
of earthworm (*Allolobophora chlorotica*). The eggs are laid on the soil
under leaves and hatch in one week. When the young larva comes into
contact with a worm it bores through the cuticle and develops inside the
worm's body. In the spring the worm's cuticle is again perforated in order
that the spiracles of the larva can obtain sufficient air. The fully-grown

larva leaves the body of the worm which is by now almost completely devoured. From this point onwards complete development takes 10 weeks. Overwintering takes place as the first-stage larvae or the hibernating adults. A second generation probably takes place during the late summer. In the autumn the adult flies may often be seen in very large numbers sunning themselves on stumps or walls. Later they find sheltered places for hibernation.

Economic importance. The Cluster Fly is so named on account of its habit of forming compact 'clusters' of hibernating individuals in buildings,

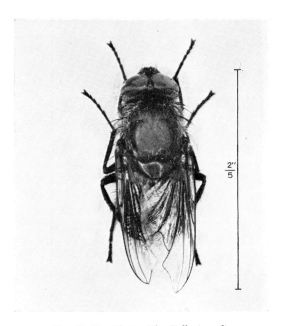

Fig. 49. The Cluster Fly, *Pollenia rudis.*

usually in upper rooms, attics or little-used rooms. They remain immobile unless an increase in temperature takes place, when they 'buzz' about and cause considerable annoyance. They do no damage to buildings except that they cause a certain amount of staining on paintwork and paper. They can gain access to the attic spaces through very small cracks or spaces under tiles. Several species of 'swarming' fly may be found in the situations described above, but *Pollenia rudis* is probably the most common and the writer believes that it is of considerably more importance during the last few years than formerly was the case. It is said that large clusters of this species give off a sweetish smell when disturbed.

The Window Gnat, *Anisopus fenestralis.* (See Fig. 50)

This species is one of a number of dipterous flies which collectively are known as 'filter flies'. They breed in sewage filters where they perform a beneficial function by preventing the fungal mat becoming too dense and clogging the filter beds in sewage works. The numbers present vary with the season but often in summer these flies breed in such profusion that they become a menace to neighbouring areas by invading houses and hampering workers out of doors. The filter flies breed and develop in the biological film of the filter, feeding upon the complex sludge of algae, fungi and bacteria which is broken down into small faecal pellets that are more easily removed by water.

Anisopus fenestralis belongs to the family ANISOPODIDAE.

Fig. 50. The Window Gnat, *Anisopus fenestralis.*

Appearance. The gnat-like fly is about 8 mm. in length and the wings bear a dark cloud-like area at the tips.

Life-cycle. Anisopus fenestralis breeds in a variety of decaying vegetation and the adults which enter houses quite fortuitously will lay their eggs on rotting fruit and vegetables as well as on moist food of various kinds. The larva has been reported as causing damage to honeycombs, cider and home-made wines. As previously mentioned, this fly normally lays her eggs on the biological films of filter-beds in sewage works. These eggs are laid in a ribbon of 150 which form a large grey spherical mass from which the young active larvae hatch in 4 days. They are brown in colour and grow to a length of 20 mm. in about 20 days. The pupal period lasts 8 days and the pupa is capable of a limited amount of movement and shifts itself to a drier situation from which emergence takes place. The adult flies live for about 7 days.

Economic importance. This fly often appears in numbers in houses, especially in the neighbourhood of sewage works, but is by no means confined to such situations. It enters dwellings accidentally, and as it is attracted to light, flies to the window where it sits about lethargically and may often be mistaken for a mosquito.

The Yellow Swarming Fly, *Thaumatomyia notata*

This is another species of house swarming fly but is classified in the family CHLOROPIDAE.

Appearance. This small yellow fly has black markings, longitudinal on the thorax and transverse on the abdomen. The abdomen is deep and the wings are rounded.

Life-cycle. Little is known concerning the developmental stages of this fly but it is recorded as being bred from several species of grasses.

Economic importance. This is one of the more common swarming flies which hibernate in attics and little-used rooms. A cluster of 12 to 14 millions of this species was once collected.

Fig. 51. The Common House Fly, *Musca domestica.*

$$\frac{1''}{4}$$

Common House Fly, *Musca domestica.* (See Fig. 51)

This species is probably the most familiar and certainly the most widely distributed of all insects. It has accompanied man everywhere and has adapted itself to breeding in a wide variety of rejected food and excrement of man and his domestic animals. This species is classified in the family MUSCIDAE in which are placed a number of seemingly diverse forms with an even more diverse range of biology.

Appearance. The adult flies are about ¼ in. in length and greyish in colour, with four narrow black stripes on the thorax.

Life-cycle. The eggs are laid in almost any vegetable or animal matter provided that it is not too dry and can be readily swallowed and digested by the larvae. Stacks of fermenting horse-dung are frequently used for breeding but this will take place also quite freely in human faeces, pig-dung and household refuse in unemptied dustbins. When egg-laying takes place in dung the latter must not be more than 72 hours old. Adult flies live from 4 to 12 weeks but the main broods are not usually in evidence before June and are more numerous in August and September. In the British Isles breeding normally ceases in October and the species over-

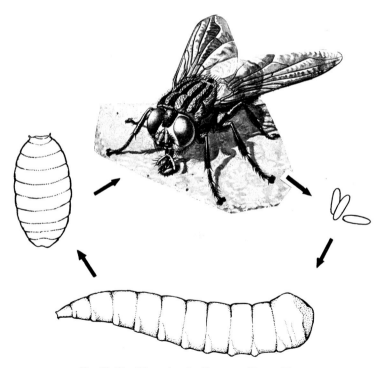

Fig. 52. The life-cycle of a Common House Fly.

winters in the larval or pupal stages, although in warm conditions a few adults may survive the winter. In the early summer there is a rapid re-colonization of all available breeding sites (see Fig. 52).

The egg. The eggs are about 1 mm. long, glistening white, and are laid in batches of 120 to 150 by the female fly, which may eventually produce a total of 600 to 900 eggs over a period of from 4 to 12 days. The time taken for the eggs to hatch varies according to temperature from about 8 hours to 3 days.

The larva. The larva is white, legless and conical in shape, tapering at the head end. In warm weather it may be fully developed in 3 days, reaching 10 to 12 mm. in length, but under less satisfactory conditions it may take 8 weeks to complete its development. When fully fed, the *maggot*, as the larva is known, appears waxy and ivory yellow in colour, and it abandons its larval environment in search of a cooler and drier place in which to pupate. The larva may travel considerable distances before it finds a suitable spot and will readily crawl up a smooth vertical surface if it is moist.

The pupa. Pupation usually takes place in the soil where the larva may bury itself to a depth of from 3 to 24 inches, depending on its nature. The pupa is formed within the last larval skin and is barrel-shaped with rounded ends. It is at first pale yellow in colour but then darkens to reddish-brown and finally to dark brown or black. The pupal period varies from 3 to 28 days according to temperature. The total time taken to complete the life-cycle varies considerably with the temperature, humidity and the nature and abundance of the food supply.

Economic importance. It would be difficult to exaggerate the importance of the Common House Fly as a pest in the homes of Britain. This is on account of its importance as a carrier of disease brought about by its habit of flying between human faeces and human food. The disease organisms of typhoid, dysentry, summer diarrhoea, probably infantile paralysis and other diseases are transferred from faecal matter to food by vomit drops, in fly excrement or by organisms adhering to the fly's feet. The eggs of parasitic worms are also transferred in this latter way. In tropical and sub-tropical areas, in addition to these diseases, the House Fly is responsible for the spread of cholera, yaws and ophthalmia. The adult fly feeds on both solid and liquid matter which can be lapped up by the sponge-like proboscis; the familiar 'fly-spots' are drops of liquid regurgitated and deposited on the surface by the fly.

The Lesser House Fly, *Fannia canicularis.* (See Fig. 53)

Appearance. The adult flies are considerably smaller than those of *Musca domestica*, measuring about $\frac{3}{10}$ in. in length. In both sexes the thorax is marked with three indistinct dark stripes. The abdomen of the female is ovoid in shape and grey in colour, whilst that of the male is narrow and tapering and blackish in colour with pale yellow semi-transparent patches.

Life-cycle

The egg. The female lays her eggs on decomposing organic matter such as decaying vegetables, fruit, fungi, rotting wood, human faecal matter and cow-dung. A semi-liquid medium is often chosen and both eggs and larvae

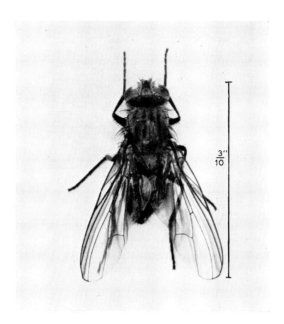

Fig. 53. Lesser House Fly, *Fannia canicularis*.

are suitably adapted for life in this special environment. A batch of eggs may consist of up to 50 and the eggs have two float-like appendages which enable them to remain suspended on the surface if the food material is semi-liquid in consistency.

The larva. The eggs hatch within 24 hours, according to temperature, and the larvae burrow into their food medium. They are slightly flattened and bear characteristic processes on which are borne fine whip-like hairs which serve to propel the larva through the semi-liquid medium. The larvae mature in approximately 7 days in summer, but this period may be extended to 3 or 4 weeks under adverse conditions.

The pupa. When fully fed the larva crawls away from the food and pupates nearby, but never deeply in the soil. Pupation takes place in the third larval skin and at this stage it can easily be mistaken for a dead larva as it may remain thus for 1 to 4 weeks before the adult emerges.

Economic importance. This species is only a little less frequent in houses than the Common House Fly (*Musca domestica*). It enters dwellings during the summer months but compared with the latter species it prefers a cooler environment and thus is active over a slightly lower temperature range. The males are more commonly found indoors than the females and their characteristic way of flying erratically in circles below pendant lamps is a well-known phenomenon. The females are often found in buildings housing cows, horses and poultry, seeking suitable oviposition sites. The Lesser House Fly is less prone to settle on foodstuffs and is consequently less liable to spread disease than the Common House Fly, but the housewife is not likely to discriminate between the species and is sure to consider all flies indoors as obnoxious.

The Blue Bottle, *Calliphora erythrocephala* and *C. vomitoria*. (See Figs. 54 and 55)

Two species as indicated above, are known by the common name of Blue Bottle, the first named being the most common. They are classified in the family CALLIPHORIDAE, together with a number of common flies such as the Green Bottles *Lucilia sericata* and *L. caesar* and the Flesh Fly *Sarcophaga carnaria*. All these are known as 'blowflies' on account of their habit of 'blowing' or depositing their eggs on exposed meat. Neither the Green Bottle nor the Flesh Fly can be said to be common household pests although both occasionally enter houses during hot weather in summer, but this is probably accidental. When they are seen indoors they are

Fig. 54. The Blue Bottle, *Calliphora erythrocephala*.

endeavouring to get out again through the glass windows as they prefer bright sunlight. Green Bottles lay their eggs on decaying animal matter and also often on open wounds of animals or in the fleece of sheep, especially around the tail if it is soiled. The householder usually encounters the Flesh Fly around the dustbins in summer when the sun is hot. In colour it is chequered black and grey and in size is about the same or slightly larger than the Blue Bottle. The female does not lay eggs but deposits first-stage

$\frac{7''}{20}$

Fig. 55. The Green Bottle, *Lucilia caesar*.

larvae, a fact sometimes observed by the housewife when, in squashing one on the window-sill, she is disgusted to find a number of small squirming maggots. The life-cycle is rapid, taking only 13 to 25 days to complete.

The following account deals with the Blue Bottle.

Appearance. The adult fly is larger and much more robust than the House Fly. It has a shiny blue body dusted with white on the abdomen which also shows lighter blue reflections.

Life-cycle. Eggs are laid by the female on flesh or dead animals and it is thought that she is attracted to the site by smell. The eggs are creamy white and about 1·5 mm. in length. Up to 600 eggs may be laid by one female. The eggs hatch in 18 to 48 hours at a temperature of 18° to 20°C. The small larvae known as maggots feed on the flesh and in doing so bore into it. At the same temperature the larval period lasts 8 to 11 days and the larva may reach a length of 18 mm.

Out of doors if a carcase is infested the fully fed larvae tunnel into the soil in its vicinity to a depth of one to a little more than six inches and there pupate. The pupal stage at 18° to 20°C. lasts from 9 to 12 days. The pupa is dull red-brown in colour and is cylindrical with rounded ends. The total length of the life cycle varies from 16 to 35 days according to temperature. During the summer months the adult stage lasts about 35 days.

Economic importance. Although the normal habitat of the Blue Bottle is out of doors, the female will enter houses with a loud buzzing noise, searching for flesh for an oviposition site or for food. In their search for meat the Blue Bottles will fly around cool, dark larders shunned by the House Fly. The larvae will also develop in household dustbins containing meat and fish scraps. This insect is looked upon with loathing by the housewife on account of her anxieties when this loud-buzzing fly enters her home.

The Seaweed Fly, *Coelopa frigida*

Appearance. The Seaweed Fly and its near relatives in the family COELO-PIDAE, are small to medium-sized, rather bristly flies with small eyes and stout legs. The last segment of the tarsus is enlarged.

Life-cycle. Little appears to be known concerning the length of the different life-stages and the biology of this insect. The adult flies may be found on the seashore throughout the year when the weather is suitable, but during the summer they are found in great numbers around seaweed cast up on the shore. The larvae breed in the seaweed, but the precise nature of their food is uncertain.

Economic importance. The Seaweed Fly is a very abundant insect found around the whole length of the coast-line wherever dead seaweed is to be found on the high-tide marks. On the seashore they are sometimes present in such numbers as to present a nuisance to visitors to seaside resorts and they often move up and down the shore in swarms. This is the reason for their inclusion in this book as they will often enter houses in coastal areas in very large numbers and thus constitute a grave nuisance. It is known that certain aromatic substances such as trichlorethylene are particularly attractive to them and they are often found in dry cleaners establishments, chemists shops and other buildings where these aromatic substances are in use.

Fruit Flies, Vinegar Flies, *Drosophila* spp. (See Fig. 56)

The genus Drosophila in the family DROSOPHILIDAE contains a number of small flies which are attracted to fermenting substances, either the more or less pure products of a fermentation process such as beer, cider, wine and vinegar, or the raw origins, such as decaying fruit and other vegetable substances. About four species are common and widely distributed and another species, *D. repleta*, which, although only recorded in the United Kingdom for the first time in 1942, is established in the London area.

Appearance. These small or very small flies are yellowish or brownish in colour with bright red eyes. Their bodies have a bulbous appearance. The householder may easily identify them by their flight which is slow and hovering, with the wing-beats so rapid that they are nearly invisible. The abdomen is easily seen hanging downwards as though the wings can hardly support the weight.

Fig. 56. The Fruit Fly, *Drosophila*.

Life-cycle. Most research work has been carried out on the cosmopolitan species *D. melanogaster* because it has been used in many countries as a laboratory insect on account of its brief life-cycle and the large size of certain cells in its salivary glands making it very useful in genetical experiments. Although it is not so common in Britain as some of the other species, the information below referring to this species may be taken as representing all British fruit flies.

Fifteen to 25 small white eggs are laid each day by the female until a total of some 400 to 900 are laid. When the larvae hatch they burrow into the food material and do not emerge until they are ready for pupation. There are three larval stages. Both the eggs, larvae and pupae are adapted for life in a semi-liquid medium such as rotting fruit. The eggs bear long filamentous processes at one end, the rear spiracles of the larvae are borne on retractile processes and the pupae bear respiratory horns with plum-like tips at the anterior end.

Length of life-cycle. The length of the complete life-cycle at 30° C. is only 7½ days! At 25° C. it is 10 days, at 20° C. it is 14 days, and at 15° C. it is 30 days. The length of the adult life varies from 13 days at 30° C. to 120 days at 10° C.

Economic importance. These flies are often a source of annoyance in the household due to their attraction towards fermented liquids. They are often found flying around during cocktails and the host may be worried if a guest has to fish out a fly from his glass. These 'wine' flies are the species *D. funebris*, *D. fenestrarum*, *D. fasciata* and *D. obscura*. The species *D. repleta* already mentioned often constitutes a serious nuisance in kitchens, canteens and hospitals. The development stages of this latter species are passed in rotting onions, cabbages and other vegetables and the adult flies sometimes settle in large numbers on exposed foods. The adults of all species are known also to settle on and probably imbibe moisture from faecal matter so that there is a strong suspicion that they may be implicated in the spread of disease.

The Green Cluster Fly, *Dasyphora cyanella*

This species belongs to the MUSCIDAE

Appearance. This species is very like the Green Bottle and can only be identified from species of *Lucilia* with difficulty. It is generally a little smaller, however, than the Green Bottles of the family CALLIPHORIDAE. It is metallic blue-green in colour when first emerged but turns more reddish as it gets older. The front part of the thorax is dusted with white.

Life-cycle. Little seems to be known of the biology of this insect except that the larvae develop in decaying matter, especially dung, in fields.

Economic importance. This is another species of swarming fly; hibernating in attics and roof spaces in a manner similar to *Pollenia rudis*.

Crane Flies, TIPULIDAE. (See Fig. 57)

Crane Flies, or 'Daddy-Long-Legs' as they are popularly known, are the adults of the well-known 'Leather Jackets'. They are classified in the family TIPULIDAE which is thought to be the most primitive family in the DIPTERA. About 90 different species in the subfamily TIPULINAE are found in Britain and those species with which we are concerned belong to this group.

Appearance. Crane Flies have long slender bodies which are often pointed at the end in the case of females. The wings are long, narrow and often clouded or barred. The antennae are thread-like and the legs also are very long and easily break off. The colour of the thorax varies with species and may be light grey to black with yellow bands. Crane Flies vary greatly

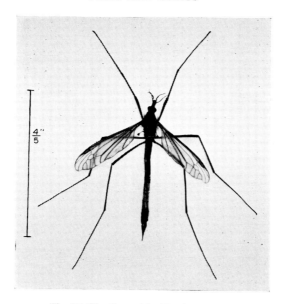

Fig. 57. The Crane Fly, *Tipula paludosa.*

in size but on the whole they are large flies and indeed include the largest British fly. The balancers are prominent.

Life-cycle. Tipula paludosa is a common Crane Fly and the following account concerns this species which may be taken as a general example. The female lays her eggs by inserting her long pointed egg-laying tube vertically in the earth, forcing it in by means of a twisting motion. Several hundred black, seed-like eggs may be laid by one female. The small grey larvae hatch from the eggs in about a fortnight and they feed on roots and underground stems. Sometimes they are so numerous in grassland that the grass is killed, leaving bare patches of earth. The larvae grow to a large size, measuring up to 40 mm., and the larval cuticle is tough, hence 'Leather Jackets'. The head can be retracted into the thoracic region. The larva pupates in May and an examination of the pupa shows the adult appendages quite clearly. A pair of respiratory horns are present on the pupal thorax. Around the abdominal segments are series of backwards-directed spines, and by means of these, the pupa is able to make its way to the surface just prior to emergence of the adult. Pupal skins projecting from the earth can easily be observed in June.

Economic importance. Crane Flies enter houses accidentally. They are sometimes present in such numbers that many fly through windows and open doors and then are unable to find their way out again. They cause no damage of any sort indoors but are a source of annoyance.

Mosquitoes, CULICIDAE

There are two main groups of mosquitoes as follows:

CULICINE, which are painful biters and capable of transmitting certain diseases found in some tropical areas; such as yellow fever, filariasis and dengue fever. This is by far the larger group.

ANOPHELINE, which are of great importance due to the fact that certain species of this group are capable of transmitting malaria.

Appearance. Mosquitoes are fairly small flies, their general appearance being well known to almost everyone. The head, of which a large part is taken up with compound eyes, is small and globular and bears a long thin proboscis and a pair of antennae which are hairy in the female and feathery or bushy in the male. The thorax is deep but thin and the wings are long and narrow and held along the body when the insect is at rest. A characteristic of the wings of mosquitoes is the presence of small scales along the veins of the wing and along its hind margin. The legs are long and thin and the body is held in a perched position when at rest. The abdomen is long and thin.

Adults of the two groups may be identified as follows:

CULICINE. Females with short palps. Abdomen covered with scales. When at rest abdomen is parallel with surface and makes an obtuse angle with head and proboscis.

ANOPHELINE. Females with palps as long as the proboscis. No scales on abdomen. When at rest proboscis and abdomen are held in a straight line which is at an angle to the surface.

Life-cycle. The immature stages of all mosquitoes are aquatic but the different species require very specific environments. Some species breed only in tree-root holes, others in stagnant ponds or salt marshes and others are found only in mountain streams.

The egg. These are spindle shaped and between 2 and 3 mm. in length. They hatch only in water but whereas some species fail to hatch if they do not come into contact with water within a few days, some desert-living forms are said to be able to hatch even after several years desiccation and they hatch within a day or so after rain has fallen. Some differences between the two groups are as follows:

CULICINE. In some species the eggs adhere vertically to form rafts, sometimes consisting of several hundred eggs. They do not possess floats.

ANOPHELINE. Eggs are laid separately on water surface but in certain species they may group together in triangles. The eggs are provided with projecting floats situated at the centre of the long axis.

The larva. The head of the larva is distinct, the thorax is rather swollen whilst the abdomen is cylindrical and composed of nine segments. As will

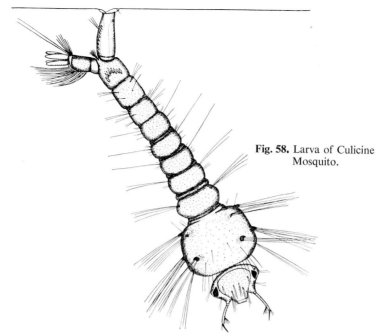

Fig. 58. Larva of Culicine Mosquito.

be seen from the illustrations there are tufts of bristles on thorax and abdomen. The head bears toothed mandibles, antennae, pigmented simple eyes and a number of bristles overhanging the mouth, known as the mouth brushes. Usually the larva feeds by filtering out of the water small organisms such as bacteria, fungal spores and pollen by means of the mouth brushes. More rarely the larva can nibble aquatic plants using the mandibles. The larva obtains its air from the atmosphere by means of spiracles situated on the eighth abdominal segment. Differences between larvae of the two groups are as follows:

CULICINE. When larva is replenishing air supply at the surface film it hangs down at an angle with only the tip of the elongated siphon in the surface film. Body bristles are simple. When at water surface larva moves by wriggling (see Fig. 58).

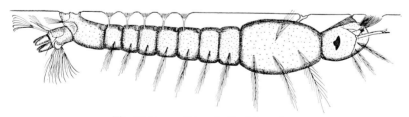

Fig. 59. Larva of Anopheline Mosquito.

ANOPHELINE. Larva is held horizontally beneath surface film by float hairs. The spiracles on the eighth abdominal segment are situated on the body surface; no siphon is present. Body bristles are feather-like. When at water surface larva moves tail first in a series of jerks (see Fig. 59).

Pupa. This is usually said to be comma-shaped. The head, thorax and curled-up legs assume a globular shape, whilst the abdomen is slender and curls forward under the thorax. The thorax bears a pair of respiratory 'trumpets' which are normally in contact with the air at the surface film but when alarmed it can dive quickly, the flexible abdomen flicking backwards and forwards, propelling the pupa in a series of jerks. When the flicking movements cease the pupa quickly surfaces on account of an air bubble situated between the rudimentary wings.

In the CULICINE group the respiratory trumpets are cylindrical.

In the ANOPHELINE they are conical.

Of the 30 British species of mosquito, 4 are Anopheline and 26 Culicine. Three 'pest' species can be said to enter houses quite commonly. They are:

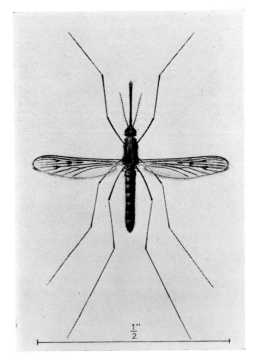

Fig. 60. *Anopheles maculipennis.*
*Reproduced by permission of the Trustees of
the British Museum.*

I. ANOPHELINE

Anopheles maculipennis. This is known as a 'domestic' species on account of the hibernation of the females in dwellings, outhouses and buildings housing domestic animals. During winter the female subsists on food reserves in its body but occasionally bites a warm-blooded animal (including man) to take a blood meal. This species exists in two forms: *messeae*, which breeds only in freshwater and is an inland insect, and *atroparvus*, which is mainly associated with brackish water and is thus coastal. It is treated as a separate species in this account (see Fig. 60).

Anopheles atroparvus. This species has only recently been separated from *A. maculipennis* with which it was included. It is brownish with small dark spots on the wings. The larvae inhabit brackish water, ditches and pools and the hibernating females which occasionally take a blood meal lay their eggs in April. Adults of the first brood appear at the end of May and there is a second and sometimes a third brood each year. It bites man freely usually at dusk or night and commonly indoors. Although its distribution is mainly coastal and estuarine it does also occur inland and this species is the most important of the European malaria carriers.

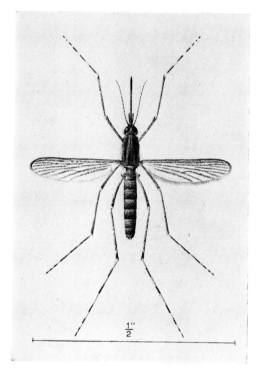

Fig. 61. *Taeniorhynchus richiardii. Reproduced by permission of the Trustees of the British Museum.*

I

II. CULICINE

Taeniorhynchus richiardii. This reddish-brown mosquito has broad pale-yellow bands on the legs and numerous pale scales on the wings. The adults appear only from May to July and it has an annual life-cycle. The females bite at dusk and during the night, and commonly enter houses. The biology of this species is exceptional amongst British mosquitoes as the larvae and pupae do not obtain their air from the atmosphere but from the tissues of aquatic plants, the roots and submerged stems of which are punctured for this purpose. The whole of the larval and pupal life is thus spent at the bottom of ponds; the pupa ascends to the surface for emergence of the adult.

In addition to the above species it should be mentioned that perhaps the most common mosquito found indoors is the 'common gnat' *Culex pipiens*, but it does not appear to bite man. It breeds in water-butts, cisterns, guttering and similar domestic situations. There are at least two generations each year, the species being most common in the autumn, although all stages die off at the onset of winter with the exception of the

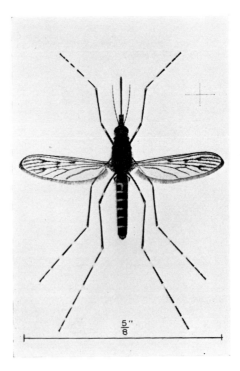

Fig. 62. *Theobaldia annulata. Reproduced by permission of the Trustees of the British Museum.*

females which hibernate. The latter emerge from their winter quarters to lay eggs in May. The adult may be identified by its rather small size, brown to reddish-brown colour with dark legs and transverse whitish bands on the abdomen. *Culex molestus* is rather similar in appearance and breeding habits to *C. pipiens* but it bites man painfully (see Fig. 61).

Theobaldia annulata is the largest native British species. It is generally common and easily recognized by the dark spots on the wings and conspicuous white bands on the legs. There are two broods and it is active until very late in the year. It often hibernates with *Culex pipiens* in cellars. It may deliver a painful bite usually at dusk. *Aedes caspius* is a biter and common in the London area, often entering houses. It is most active in the afternoons and is double-brooded (see Fig. 62).

Economic importance. It will already have been appreciated from the foregoing that the mosquito group constitutes a serious pest in houses. Many species inflict painful bites and some species do so at night when the victim is asleep. Scratching the itching bite often sets up secondary complications. Happily, malarial parasites are now no longer transmitted by them in Britain, but it should be borne in mind that this was not always the case.

I*

11

HUMAN, CAT AND DOG FLEAS

Siphonaptera

There are only about a thousand species in the order SIPHONAPTERA and although they are distributed throughout the world they exhibit a remarkable similarity in form. The adults do not develop wings but nevertheless they are thought to have been developed from rather primitive DIPTERA and to have lost their wings as a consequence of the parasitic mode of life of the adult stage. Indeed, all fleas in the adult stage are parasites of warm-blooded animals, and their extreme thinness (or lateral compression) and their backwardly directed spines allow them to move easily through fur and feathers. Another characteristic of fleas is their muscular legs; they are all good jumpers, allowing them to reach a host quickly or to make a quick escape, as most housewives who have had to cope with them will be aware.

Each separate species of flea prefers to bite and suck blood from one particular warm-blooded host, but on occasion, as when the preferred host is absent, they will bite other animals, including man. The importance to man of this habit lies in the transference of parasitic worms and pathogenic organisms to domestic animals and man.

Three species which, on occasion, may be common in dwellings are:

The Human Flea *Pulex irritans*
The Cat Flea   *Ctenocephalides felis*
The Dog Flea   *Ctenocephalides canis*

The following account concerns these three species:

Appearance. All fleas are small insects and, as previously mentioned, they are very considerably laterally compressed. This makes it difficult for the insect to run over a smooth surface but it is extremely agile when making its way through fur or clothing. Because of their flatness, the characteristic parts are only visible from the side. Fleas are reddish or chestnut brown in colour and the various segments of thorax and abdomen appear like overlapping scales. The head is fairly small and like a helmet in shape. The club-shaped antennae fit into a groove and simple eyes may or may not be present. Some species bear a row of short, thick, black spines on the under-side of the front of the head. This is known as the oral or genal comb and similarly a row may be present on the hind margin of the

132

first segment of the thorax. This is the thoracic or pronotal comb. The combs are an important aid to identification.

The Human Flea (see Figs. 63, 64 and 65) can be distinguished from Cat and Dog Fleas even with the naked eye by a sharp-sighted person. The Human Flea lacks both an oral and a pronotal comb, both of which are present in Cat and Dog Fleas. Indeed, in both these species the combs consist of stout dark-coloured, sometimes almost black, bristles and even though the individual bristles are not readily visible, the black areas can be made out. The identification of Cat and Dog Flea is more difficult and would involve the use of a microscope, but the head of the Cat Flea (see Fig. 66) is more elongated and not rounded at the front when compared with the head of the Dog Flea.

Fig. 63. The Human Flea, *Pulex irritans*.

The Dog Flea occurs on dogs and foxes and occasionally on cats. It is a common flea as is also the Cat Flea, which also is sometimes found on dogs. The Cat Flea readily bites man and is often the species found in severe infestations in dwellings.

Both males and females suck blood which is accomplished by the sharp sword-shaped mandibles and the grooved labrum. The inner sides of the mandibles and the labrum form the channel, saliva runs down into the wound and the blood is sucked out by a pump mechanism situated in the throat. Some of the blood passes into the mid-gut and part passes directly into the rectum to be evacuated undigested. It is this latter blood which forms an important part of the diet of the larva.

The legs of the flea are strong and muscular and adapted for jumping and there are strong claws present for clinging; nevertheless fleas are not able to jump upwards more than 5 or 6 inches.

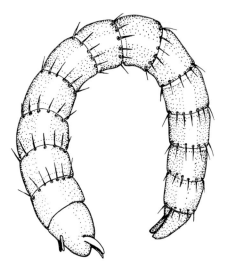

Fig. 64. Larva of Human Flea, *Pulex irritans*.

Life-cycle

The egg. Eggs are laid in the fur, feathers, clothing or sleeping place of the host. They are pearly-white and oval and although very small, measuring about 0·5 mm. in length, they can be distinguished by the naked eye. They are laid on the fur or clothing of the host but soon drop off around the host's sleeping place. Four to 8 eggs are laid after each blood meal and the total number of eggs laid may reach several hundred.

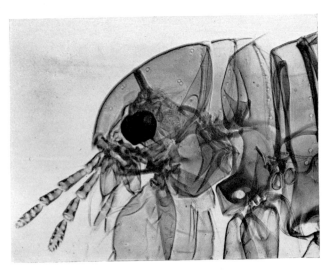

Fig. 65. Head of Human Flea, *Pulex irritans*.

The larva. The larvae are white and legless, about 1·5 mm. in length when first hatched but growing to about 5 mm. when ready to pupate. They are thread-like with a distinguishable head, three thoracic and ten abdominal segments. Eyes are absent but a pair of toothed mandibles are present and a number of backwardly-directed bristles are borne on each segment. The larva is able to wriggle about by means of the bristles and the pair of foot-like processes borne on the last abdominal segment. The food of the larva consists of a mixture of organic debris likely to be present in the host animal's sleeping quarters of which the most important element is the partly digested blood present in the faeces of the adult fleas, particles of waste food and the host's faecal matter. After passing through three stages the larva spins a silken cocoon to which particles of dirt adhere and in this the change to the pupa takes place.

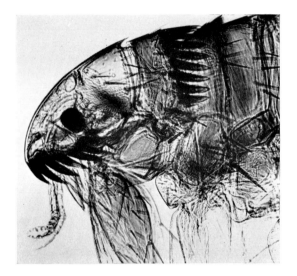

Fig. 66. Head of Cat Flea, *Ctenocephalides felis.*

The pupa. This is at first creamy-white but later turns brownish. The various parts of the adult flea are easily made out. An interesting adaption to its mode of life is the adult emergence from the cocoon. This does not take place immediately on the final metamorphosis from pupa to adult but only with the vibrations caused by the host's visit to the pupal site, usually the sleeping quarters. This is the reason for the large-scale flea attacks which sometimes take place when a person is visiting an old house where, for example, a cat has been sleeping. The vibrations caused by the persons footfalls on the floorboards is sufficient to cause considerable numbers of fleas to break through the cocoons and seek their new host by jumping.

Length of life-cycle. The egg hatches in about one week at normal room temperature and the larva of *Pulex*, at 23°C., takes 19 days to complete its development. It is thought that the complete life-cycle during summer in Britain takes about one month. During winter the life-cycle would be very much prolonged. At 10°C. the larva takes 105 days to complete this stage.

Economic importance. Fleas are generally considered to be disgusting creatures and apart from the physical discomfort caused by their bites they are the source of considerable annoyance as well as anxiety. Although the Human Flea *Pulex irritans* is not usually the carrier of pathogenic organisms, two diseases, plague and murine typhus, are transmitted by the bites of the tropical Rat Flea *Xenopsylla cheopis*, which will readily bite man. In addition, fleas are implicated in the transference of the immature stages of tapeworms. Flea larvae may swallow the eggs of the dog tapeworm *Dipylidium caninum* when they are devouring faecal matter. The parasitized flea is then swallowed by a dog nuzzling its fur to allay irritation. The worm is then at the cysterceroid stage ('bladder-worm') but it develops to the adult stage in the dog.

12

THE WOOD LOUSE AND CENTIPEDE

Some non-insect pests

In spite of the title of this book, this chapter is devoted to Arthropods other than Insects which may enter houses and often cause some concern. There are three classes as follows:

Class: CRUSTACEA. This group consists of the crabs, lobsters, shrimps and related animals including the wood lice. Three common species of wood lice are noted.

Class: CHILOPODA. These are the centipedes, and although they cannot be said to be very common indoors when they do intrude into the household they cause consternation and sometimes fear. Notes are given on two common species.

Class: ARACHNIDA. Spiders and mites constitute this group. Spiders found in the home cannot truthfully be called pests although they may be looked upon with some distaste by the fastidious house-wife. They will probably be preying upon insects and therefore playing a beneficial role. Several species of mites are, however, serious pests and five species will be described.

CRUSTACEA. The members of this class differ from insects, spiders and other classes that together constitute the Phylum *Arthropoda*, in possessing two pairs of antennae, at least three pairs of mouth parts, breathing by means of gills or by the general body surface and by, in almost all cases, being of aquatic habit. The members of this group that enter houses, however, are not aquatic. They are known by the popular name of wood lice.

Wood lice belong to the order ISOPODA. Their arched bodies are oval when looked at from above. A feature distinguishing wood lice from crabs and lobsters is that the eyes are not situated on a stalk. The antennae are relatively large and consist of an elbowed peduncle and a whip-like flagellum. Preceding the antennae is a pair of much smaller antennules. The thorax consists of seven segments each of which bears a pair of walking legs and the abdomen consists of six segments, each with a pair of append-ages known as pleopods, with the exception of the last pair which are known as uropods. The wood lice are the only truly terrestrial crustaceans and even so the great hazard to their survival is desiccation. They are always found in cool, damp and usually dark situations such as under stones, under bark and dead leaves and similar sites. There are 38 species in Britain of which 3 very common species, *Oniscus asellus*, *Porcellio scaber* and *Armadillidium vulgare*, enter houses fortuitously during darkness and then are unable to escape. They often crawl up the overflow or waste pipes into the bathroom and then cannot escape from the bath, or they are attracted to the damp spots in the kitchen such as under the sink. They feed on heavily decayed wood and other soft vegetable debris and cause no damage indoors.

Fig. 67. The Wood Louse, *Oniscus asellus*.

Oniscus asellus may be 15 mm. in length and 7·5 mm. in width. The integument is slightly shiny and the colour is slaty grey with irregular lighter markings. It is one of the largest and commonest of the British wood lice (see Fig. 67).

Porcellio scaber is 17 mm. and twice as long as wide. The integument is covered with tubercles which gives it a matt appearance and this character serves to distinguish it from *Oniscus asellus*.

Armadillidium vulgare: this is another large wood louse growing up to 18 mm. in length and is a little more than twice as long as broad. In colour it is rather variable and although usually of a light grey shade, black or yellow individuals may be observed. This species is often called the pill wood louse on account of its ability to roll up into a ball on being disturbed. It requires a chalky diet and is usually only common in chalky or limestone districts.

Centipedes, CHILOPODA

Centipedes are elongate animals with the body divided into a number of, for the most part, similar segments. Each segment, which is somewhat flattened, bears a pair of limbs used for locomotion. A pair of antennae and three pairs of mouth parts arise from the head. A pair of poison claws are borne on the under surface of the first body segment lying immediately behind the head. The centipede seizes and pierces its prey with the claws and then injects venom into the wounds. The various species differ in the number of legs which they possess. The lowest number is 15 pairs and the highest over a 100 pairs.

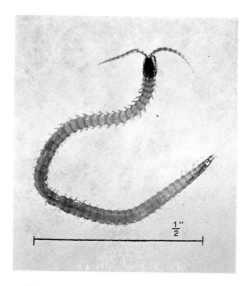

Fig. 68. The Centipede, *Necrophlaeophagus longicornis.*

The integument of centipedes lacks the waxy coating of the insect cuticle and this lowers the animal's resistence to desiccation. Centipedes are therefore always found in damp situations where they are likely to come across their prey such as worms, insects and wood lice. Hiding by day in the earth, under loose bark of fallen trees or amongst fallen leaves and vegetable debris, they wander forth at night. It is at this time that they make their way into dwellings, quite accidentally, under doors or through gaps in windows or up water pipes into the kitchen sink or the bathroom. They have been found in beds but it is certain that this is only an effort to find a dark humid situation in which to await nightfall and the centipede gets trapped between the sheets. None of the common British species are likely to produce enough venom to harm a human being, and even the large tropical species have a reputation for the vicious use of their poison glands far in excess of fact.

Notes on two common British species likely to be found indoors in the above-mentioned situations are given below:

Necrophlaeophagus longicornis. This is a long thin centipede with the segments of the antennae long and hairy. It grows to 44 mm. in length and the number of pairs of legs vary from 41 to 53 in the males and 43 to 57 in the females. It is yellowish in colour and always appears to hold its body in a loosely looped condition as in the illustration, and when moving is winding itself out of one set of loops and into another. Centipedes are thought to live for some years and indeed some individuals may not

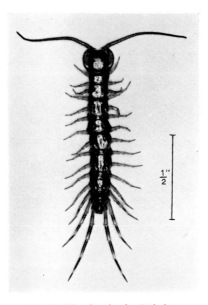

Fig. 69. The Centipede, *Lithobius variegatus.*

become mature until their third summer. The females exhibit strong maternal feelings, tending the batch of 25 to 45 eggs, and the young when they hatch until they are able to look after themselves (see Fig. 68).

Lithobius forficatus. This is a large species growing to a length of from 18 to 32 mm. It is dark brown and the body is stout and shining. In contrast to the previous species there are 15 pairs of legs only and the young hatch from the egg with only 7 pairs. *L. forficatus* is more usually found in houses in dark, damp places in the kitchen such as under the sink than elsewhere. Being stouter than the first-named species it is not able to creep in through such small cracks and orifices.

13

MITES AND TICKS

Furniture Mites—Flour Mite—Scabies (itch) Mite—Sheep Ticks

Acari

Mites and Ticks, ACARI

Mites and ticks constitute the order ACARI which is included with the spiders, scorpions and allied groups in the class ARACHNIDA. Mites show some similarity to insects in that they have jointed legs and an exoskeleton, but whereas adult insects possess six legs adult mites possess eight. Again, the bodies of insects show a substantial degree of segmentation whereas the bodies of mites are unsegmented, appearing rather bag-like. There is no division into head, thorax and abdomen as occurs in insects or into cephalothorax and abdomen as in spiders. Mites pass through an immature, larval stage in which six legs only are present and this serves to separate mites from all other orders in the ARACHNIDA.

Mites are present in very great numbers in the soil and are present also in a wide range of habitat and environment. Their small and even minute size, however, renders them normally invisible to the householder.

Many mites are parasites of plants and animals and certain species are parasites of man. Other species infest foodstuffs and are often of economic importance in food-processing factories and warehouses. An account is given below of six species of relatively common occurrence in the household or species which may be common in special circumstances.

The House Mite or Furniture Mite, *Glycyphagus domesticus*. (See Fig. 70)

Appearance. The male varies from 0·32 to 0·40 mm. and the female from 0·40 to 0·75 mm. The legs are long and fairly slender and, situated at the hinder end of the female, there is a short tube-like organ. The setae borne on the upper-side are long and somewhat feather-like. As will be seen from the figure the mite has a somewhat hexagonal appearance.

Life-cycle. The eggs hatch in about 5 days into six-legged wrinkled larvae which feed for 2 days before becoming swollen and shining. They rest for two days and then moult. The resulting stage is known as a protonymph which feeds for 4 days, rests for a further 2 days and moults again. The next stage is known as the deutonymph which lasts for 5 days spent in activity, followed by a further 2 days resting. The final moult then transforms it into the adult. Some individuals are capable of resisting adverse conditions by assuming a special form known as a hypopus. This is devoid of appendages and is cyst-like, being enclosed within the skin of the proto-nymph. It may remain in the hypopal form for as long as six months.

Economic importance. This widely distributed mite is commonly found infesting foodstuffs of many kinds and, in addition, it is often found on furniture in damp, ill-ventilated rooms and especially on upholstered furniture filled with 'Green Algerian fibre'. When found on furnishings it is thought to be feeding on surface growing fungi.

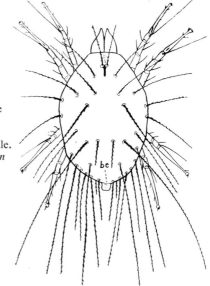

Fig. 70. The House Mite or Furniture Mite, *Glycyphagus domesticus.* Dorsal view of the female. *Reproduced by permission of the Trustees of the British Museum.*

The Flour Mite, *Acarus siro* (previously known as *Tyroglyphus farinae*). (See Fig. 71)

Appearance. The male measures from 0·32 to 0·40 mm. and the female from 0·35 to 0·65 mm. in length. The fore-part of the pearly white body is conical and the hinder part oval with a distinct groove separating the two parts. Except for a pair of setae situated at the hinder end of the body, the setae are not nearly so long as those of the House Mite and only four setae borne on the conical region are feather-like. The legs are only moderately long and are brown in colour.

A hypopal stage is sometimes present, the shape of which is more rounded than that of the adult. The surface is covered with minute cavities and there is a sucker plate on the under-surface. This stage is about 0·20 mm. in length.

Life-cycle. This is similar to that of the House Mite in most respects. The hypopus does not feed but is a distributive phase accomplished by attaching itself to insects by the sucker plate. The total length of the life-cycle is from 2 to 4 weeks if hypopal stage is undertaken.

Economic importance. This is considered to be one of the most serious pests of stored food products. Flour, cereals and cereal products, cheese and dried fruits are the most commonly infested materials, and the mites may often be present in the larder. When this mite is present in large numbers in produce, it is known to cause dermatitis when it is handled and digestive disorders have been recorded from persons consuming infested foodstuff. Infested material may often be identified by the 'mite dust' around it and

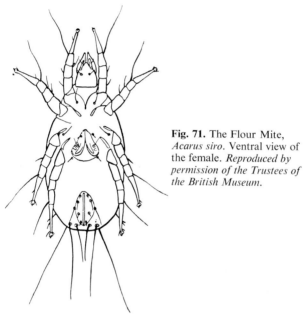

Fig. 71. The Flour Mite, *Acarus siro.* Ventral view of the female. *Reproduced by permission of the Trustees of the British Museum.*

the mites themselves give off a 'minty' smell. The Flour Mite is preyed on by another mite, *Cheyletus,* which, in some circumstances, can effect a reasonable control.

The Itch Mite, *Sarcoptes scabiei.* (See Fig. 72)

A number of mites classified in the family SARCOPTIDAE are parasites of the skin of man and animals. In domestic animals these mites cause skin diseases known as mange and on occasion they may be transmitted to persons who are in close contact with dogs and other animals. The very unpleasant human disease known as *scabies,* is caused by the mite *Sarcoptes scabiei.*

Appearance. The shape of the body of this mite is roundish-oval, rounded above and flat beneath, and in colour it is pearly-grey. The male measures about 0·23 mm. in length and the female 0·33 to 0·45 mm. It is possible to separate the male from the female on account of the stumpy legs: in both sexes the first two pairs of legs terminate in a long, stalked, sucker-like organ. In the female, the third and fourth pair of legs bear a long whip-like seta, whereas in the male these are borne on the third pair only, those of the fourth bearing the sucker-like organs of the first and second pair.

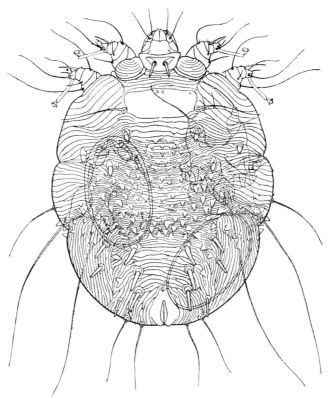

Fig. 72. The Itch Mite, *Sarcoptes scabiei*. Dorsal view of the female.
Reproduced by permission of the Trustees of the British Museum.

Life-cycle. One to three white, glossy eggs per day measuring only 0·09 to 0·17 mm. are laid by the adult female as she constructs a meandering burrow in the horny layer of the skin. The gallery so made may be up to three-quarters of an inch in length. The eggs hatch in two or three days into a larva with six legs which lives, in part, on the surface of the skin. It moults into a nymph with eight legs after a lapse of two or three days, and this again lives partly on the skin surface. A certain amount of exploratory wandering takes place and the nymph may rest from time to time in a hair follicle. It then moults either into the adult male form or into a second-stage nymph before it finally moults into the adult female, which again burrows into the skin, forming a temporary gallery. When fertilization has been effected the female commences her permanent burrow. The whole life-cycle takes only 14 to 17 days in the case of the female and 9 to 11 days in the male.

Economic importance. Infestation by relatively few mites of the species *Sarcoptes scabiei* causes the skin disease known as scabies. Although the disease may affect all parts of the body it predominates on the limbs. An intolerable itching results from the burrowing mite which causes scratching, and secondary infections are the usual course of events. Beginning from one to six months, sensitization occurs when the skin shows a reaction to the presence of the mites by the formation of numerous small vesicles and a general erythmatous condition. This eventually causes a decline in the mite population and it is thought that the mites may eventually die out.

If a person has previously suffered from scabies, he or she is partially immune to reinfestation. If the mites do succeed in getting established they never reach a population of more than about 25. A substantial number of female mites are removed by scratching.

The scabies rash, produced by sensitization, does not correspond with the sites of mite attack but groups of vesicles about the size of a grain of wheat are often associated with the mite burrow. Secondary skin affections resulting from scratching include impetigo and eczema.

It appears that it is only the fertilized female which is capable of initiating a new scabies attack and this is most likely to occur when persons sleep together. The incidence of mite transmission by more temporary contact, caressing, hand holding or by children playing can only be guessed at, certainly it would be difficult to assess. The incidence of scabies fluctuates widely; it increased a year or two before the Second World War but it decreased sharply a few years afterwards.

The Harvest Mite, *Trombicula autumnalis.* (See Fig. 73)

The parasitic larval stage of this mite is brought indoors by its human host and in areas where this pest abounds it is a source of considerable irritation.

Appearance. The larva is six-legged and varies in colour from whitish to bright orange-red. Before feeding it is about 0·22 mm. in length but when fully fed it is about 0·6 mm. On the back of the mite there is a five-sided, shield-shaped area and a number of barbed setae. The legs bear a number of feathery hairs and terminate in three long, slender, sickle-shaped claws.

Life-cycle. The eggs are laid in soil and the larvae make their way upwards, climbing to the tips of blades of grass or to the terminal point of the leaves of low-growing shrubs. When opportunity permits it transfers to a warm-

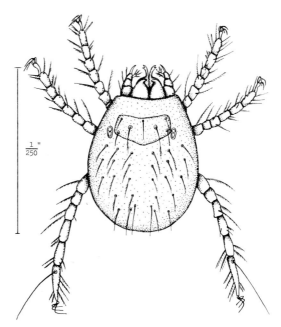

$\frac{1}{250}$ "

Fig. 73. The Harvest Mite, *Trombicula autumnalis*.

blooded animal such as a rodent, a dog, a bird or a man. The larval mite requires an area of thin skin which it first searches for and then pierces with its mouth parts. The mite injects a fluid into the wound which breaks down the cell structure immediately beneath the horny layers of the skin and it proceeds to suck up the liquid matter produced. Alternating periods of sucking and injecting go on for two or three days whilst the larva increases in size. It then drops to the ground and five or six weeks are passed before it changes to an eight-legged nymphal stage. It finally changes to the adult stage but the nymph and the adult appear to live on the surface of the ground, being mainly predaceous or scavenging in habit.

Economic importance. In certain parts of the country, particularly chalky areas such as the Chiltern Hills and certain parts of Wales, particularly the counties Cardigan and Montgomery, the Harvest Mite is a scourge to many people who work in or walk through grassy areas, especially in the vicinity of rabbit-warrens. The mite is at first unobserved and unfelt but this stage is soon followed by a period of intense irritation which lasts for a few days and often causes sleepless nights. The site of the mite attack is often where garments restrict their further crawling such as a belt at the waist or garters holding up socks. The irritation is sometimes so severe that the unfortunate person believes that the 'bug' has burrowed under the skin, but in fact the mite does not move from its original location where it first pierces the skin. Of course the biting larval stage of the mite, being immature, cannot lay eggs. It should be mentioned that some persons are not selected as hosts by the mite, perhaps in some way the mite considers them distasteful, or if attacked the bite does not set up irritation. In any case such fortunate people are immune to the harmful effects of Harvest Mite infestation.

In Eastern Asia a *Trombicula*-like mite carries and transmits to man the pathogenic organisms, a species of Rickettsia, which causes the dreaded disease known as 'scrub typhus'. This disease is unknown in Britain.

The Clover or Gooseberry Mite, *Bryobia praetiosa.* (See Fig. 74)

This mite is classified in the TETRANYCHIDAE, some species of which are horticultural pests.

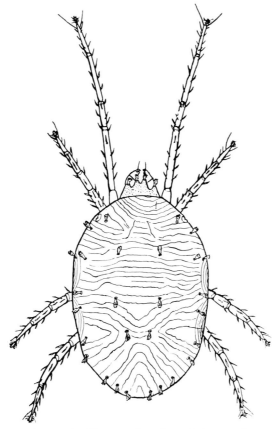

Fig. 74. The Clover or Gooseberry Mite, *Bryobia praetiosa.* Dorsal view of the female. *Reproduced by permission of the Trustees of the British Museum.*

Appearance. The body of this mite is oval in shape and varies in colour from yellowish-green to bright red. The female measures approximately 0·7 mm. in length, and although all the legs are long and slender, the first pair are by far the longest. There are two interesting minute features (which can only be seen with the aid of a microscope): the back bears a number of club-shaped setae and the claw of the first pair of legs of the female is extraordinarily complex.

Life-cycle. The globular eggs are bright red and the emerging larvae which feed on plant sap are of a similar colour. A wide range of plants have been recorded as hosts of this mite, such as various fruit-trees and bushes, ivy, various grass species and clover.

Economic importance. The importance of this mite as a pest lies in its migratory habit. It is a common occurrence, especially in the south of England, for very large numbers of ovigerous females to invade dwellings usually at the end of April to the beginning of May, but sometimes in the autumn. Why this migration into houses takes place is still a mystery, the only explanation so far given is that such invasions usually occur in recently erected houses and the mites are seeking egg-laying sites which they would normally find on tree-trunks, and hence they would endeavour to travel vertically, walls replacing trees.

Although the presence of these mites is often disturbing to the housewife they are innocuous, causing harm neither to the person nor to any material indoors.

The Grain Itch-Mite, *Pyemotes* (=*Pediculoides*) *ventricosus.* (See Fig. 75)

This mite classified in the family TARSONEMIDAE is normally beneficial as it is a parasite on a large number of different insect species, usually in their larval stage. The populations of grain pests and the ordinary woodworm are probably much reduced by the habit of the mite of fastening on to, burying its head into, and sucking the juices of, the soft-skinned insect larvae.

Appearance. This mite most usually occurs in households, infesting woodworm grubs, and if a piece of wood is broken open some woodworm larvae can often be seen with these small glistening pearl-like mites adhering to them. These are the females. The males remain on the abdomen of their mother and fertilize their sister mites as they are produced. They probably obtain some nourishment also from their mother by parasitizing her.

Economic importance. If a person handles infested grain or sometimes woodworm-infested wood an itching occurs, due to the mite embedding its head-end into the skin. (On occasion the writer has been asked if woodworm 'bite'.) Although this mite is commonly found in dwellings it rarely transfers its attacks to humans.

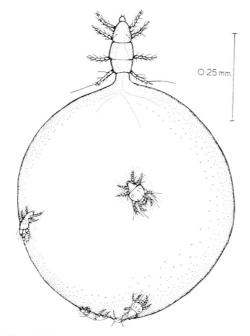

0·25 mm.

Fig. 75. The Grain Itch-Mite, *Pyemotes ventricosus.*

The Castor Bean Tick or Common Sheep Tick, *Ixodes ricinus.* (See Fig. 76)
The ticks belong to the family IXODIDAE and are much larger than mites.
They all feed on vertebrate blood although in some cases, they may only be
attached to their host for a relatively short period.

Appearance. This tick is oval in shape with a hard oval plate on the front
end of the upper surface. A characteristic organ is the *hypostome,*
bearing a number of recurved teeth so that it acts like a harpoon in being
difficult to pull out when the skin has been pierced. The female has a very
extensible skin so that when blood is imbibed the mite swells up to such an
extent that it resembles a blood blister and has the same dark purplish-grey
colour.

Life-cycle. The young ticks climb vegetation and remain waiting at the tips
of grass blades, etc., for the passage of a host on to which they transfer
themselves by means of their front legs. They require conditions of high
humidity so that after a period on a grass tip, if a host is not encountered,
they drop down to the earth to take in moisture before ascending again.

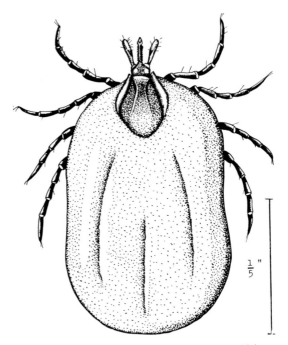

Fig. 76. The Castor Bean or Common Sheep Tick,
Ixodes ricinus.

Economic importance. This tick is often brought indoors by domestic animals, especially dogs, and in districts where they are common, they can be found between the claws or behind the ears. Ticks are known to carry many important diseases of cattle, and in countries abroad, but not in Britain, dangerous human diseases.

Part III

14

NOTES ON CONTROL

Control of insect pests in the home is an integral and important part of household management. Home hygiene, although of great importance, plays only a part in this because even though some insects may be in the house as a direct consequence of low standards of hygiene, others, such as the fortuitous wanderers and Common Furniture Beetle, are independent of hygiene standards.

However, the comparative absence or presence of insects in the home is fast becoming a measure of the standard of living enjoyed. Certainly the accelerated tempo of modern living leaves no room for anxieties concerning insect pests, the appearance of which in the home cause so much disquiet. Stemming from this is the increasing reliance on professional servicing companies for dealing with infestations of insect pests in the home. This is widespread in America where the service-man of the pest control company is just as much accepted as is the milkman.

The first essential in insect pest control is identification. When an insect is found in the home and is then correctly determined, one can immediately assess its importance, learn something of the essential features of its biology and know something of the economic damage it is likely to cause. On the other hand it may be dismissed as 'something out of the garden'. Although this book is largely concerned with identification of household insect pests the following notes on control measures are appended. There will be one important decision for the householder to make. Whether to exterminate the pest on a do-it-yourself basis or whether to call in a representative of a pest control servicing firm. These notes then, it is hoped, will help the reader to make the decision.

Factors Influencing the Choice of Insecticides for Insect Control

The choice of an insecticide for the control of a specific insect needs careful consideration for the following reasons:

1. In those insects which exist in four stages—egg, larva, pupa, adult— as a general rule the different stages differ in their susceptibility to insecticides, e.g. larvae and pupae are often more resistant than adults.

2. The mode of life of a specific insect or specific stage in the life-cycle must be taken into account, e.g. crawling, motionless and flying insects would each best be attacked by different methods.

3. The next point of consideration is whether to use a 'residual' or 'knock-

down' type of insecticide, or a combination of both. By 'residual' we mean an insecticide whose properties are long lasting, causing insects to die days, weeks or months after application even if somewhat slowly. On the other hand, the 'knockdown' type of insecticides cause an immediate paralysis of the insect, in fact it appears to be *knocked down*. These latter insecticides are generally transitory in their power, being rapidly affected by sunlight and other factors. Insecticides based on pyrethrum may be given as an example of this type. Pyrethrum is a natural material made from the ground flowers of a daisy-like plant or an oil extract is made from them.

4. In the case of residual treatment, the porosity and extent of the surface to which the insecticide is to be applied is of paramount importance in determining the kind and amount of preparation to use.

5. The presence of food, or the situation may be where food is prepared and these may impose restrictions, see below.

6. The presence of a fire, stove or naked flame may impose further restrictions. Oil-based sprays should never be used unless all such are extinguished. The same precaution applies to the large-scale use of woodworm-killing fluids.

In general the type of spray to be used is governed by the following:

1. Flying insects require sprays with high 'knockdown' effects if immediate results are required, e.g. wasps and numerous flies where food is being prepared.

2. Direct attack on insects at all stages requires an oil-based spray with good 'knockdown' properties. Oils penetrate the waxy layer of the cuticle of insects and thus the insecticidal material comes into immediate, intimate contact with the tissues of the insect.

3. Residual treatment against flying and crawling insects is best accomplished by applying to the surface upon which the insects crawl, a liquid insecticide having both residual and fumigant properties.

4. Residual treatment against larvae is best accomplished by means of a powder with toxicity as a stomach poison and with long residual effect. Large crawling insects can also be treated in this way.

5. Residual effect throughout is influenced by the type of surface to be treated, and, in general, porous surfaces should be treated with water-based emulsions or water-dispersible powder, depending on the degree of porosity of the surface. Non-porous surfaces should be treated with oil-based formulations or with resins.

6. Where food is present special care must be exercised. No insecticides should be allowed to come into contact with food, not even in the smallest quantity. Some insecticides possess strong aromatic odours which they may impart to foodstuffs, causing 'taint'. In addition, some insecticides, even though of a moderate or low order of human toxicity, are not rapidly excreted from the system and tend to concentrate in certain organs. This

means that ingestion of relatively minute amounts of such insecticides may build up to harmful proportions.

In pest control some of the hazards which must be borne in mind, and precautions which must be taken, have already been noted, but some additional points are now given.

1. Pest control chemicals must be stored where children cannot possibly get at them. For this reason, also, pest control liquids must not be decanted from their tins into receptacles such as cups, glasses or basins, which may give to young children the idea that the liquid in the cup is a drink. Many instances are known of young children drinking such liquids when their parents' attention has been diverted.

2. The disposal of residues is often a problem. Small quantities of insecticides remaining at the bottom of tins should not be left in old sheds and other places where their presence is subsequently forgotten. For the sake of safety it is worth while throwing such liquids into the drain and flushing plenty of water after it. Smash the tin so that is could not possibly be used for any other purposes and place it in the dustbin.

3. Domestic animals are sometimes harmed and even killed by their owners mistakenly applying an unsuitable insecticide to the fur of the dog or cat for control of lice or fleas. The skins of these animals are particularly susceptible to certain insecticidal substances such as some of the chlorinated hydrocarbons. They are able to pass through the skin and this may have serious results. Before applying an insecticide to a dog or a cat make sure that the manufacturers state on the container that the insecticide is suitable for this purpose.

IMPORTANT. *The most important advice that can be given to a person about to use an insecticide in the home is to make sure that the label on the container has been read with care and understood. The next most important thing is to carry out all the instructions concerning its application, carefully guard against the hazards and take all the stated precautions.*

Aerosols

Insecticides are often sold in what is now generally known as 'aerosol' form. It is important that the user of one understands how they work. The container is gas-tight and is under pressure internally. This is because the insecticide is mixed with a low-boiling point liquid, the usual boiling point being just above the freezing point of water. Thus, if, by means of a valve, an orifice is created the mixture of insecticide and gas is released under pressure and a fine spray of small droplet-size results. The valve is operated by slight pressure of the first finger when the aerosol can is held in the hand.

The aerosol is a convenient form of insecticide application and has proved popular where the amount of insecticide applied is small and where only a few insects are involved, such as small-scale direct fly control.

Where the amount of insecticide to be applied is considerable, however, application by aerosol is expensive.

Most people get the knack of operating an aerosol quite readily but there have been accidents where the spray has been directed on to the face instead of away from the body, so that before pressing the valve the position of the orifice should be noted. It is sometimes indicated by an arrow.

With an aerosol, disposal of the empty cannister may sometimes be a problem as there is sometimes some residual pressure due to the valve not having released all the propellent. Never throw it into a fire, whether indoors or outside, and do not endeavour to pierce or smash it. Make sure it is as empty as the valve will allow and put it into the dustbin.

Brief Notes on Control of Various Insect Pests

Ants

The insecticides chlordane and dieldrin have been found to be particularly effective where ants are concerned. They are used either as a spray or 'banding', painting the insecticide in a continuous band along skirtings, around radiators and piping in such a way that the ants are obliged to cross the band during their foraging operations. Another very efficacious method of ant control concerns the use of insecticidal resins or lacquers, although their use is best left to the professional servicing companies. The insecticide progressively 'blooms' or produces a minute crystal structure which is re-formed when it is removed by dusting and is stimulated by insects crawling over it. In this way the resin may remain effective for as long as two years. It is applied by brush in a similar manner and in similar situations as in 'banding'. It must not be applied, however, on absorbent surfaces or in places where grease, fat or dirt may accumulate. The solvent is inflammable and precautions should be taken to ensure that it does not ignite.

The Bed Bug

At one time fumigation with the very poisonous gas hydrogen cyanide was the only efficient method of dealing with a widespread bug infestation in a building or group of buildings. This type of control can only be carried out by highly trained personnel. In addition the residents had to be found alternative accommodation for at least one night. Today, however, the use of persistent insecticides renders fumigation unnecessary in the vast majority of cases.

The insecticide is applied liberally at about one ounce per square yard, about half a gallon being required for a bedroom. As well as the walls, under loose wallpaper, behind pictures, and under skirting boards, furniture should also be treated. This method of control has the advantage that the residents do not have to move elsewhere whilst it is being carried out and, in addition, because the insecticide used is the persistent type, it deals effectively with re-invasions from adjoining properties.

In spite of what has been said above on fumigation, it is often a good plan to send furniture away for fumigation, especially large stuffed items that would otherwise be difficult to treat by spraying.

Carpet Beetles

Infestations of these insects mostly originate in birds' nests such as those of house-sparrow, house-martin, swift and starling. The Carpet Beetle larvae subsist on the soiled wood and feathers in the nest-lining and then manage to get under the eaves into the roof space. From this situation they crawl into the upper rooms of the house, usually following the hot-water pipe system, and they appear to be attracted to warmer situations. Airing cupboards often harbour substantial infestations. Carpet Beetles do, however, sometimes fly through open windows and presumably initiate infestations directly, but infestations arising from birds' nests cause continual invasions. The first rule of control therefore is to remove birds' nests from eaves and all similar situations. If dead birds or rodents are found in chimneys or under floors they should be removed. Any pieces of old carpet or similar material in lofts or roof voids must be destroyed otherwise they will act as reservoirs of infestation.

In trunks or cases, as a deterrent application of paradichlorobenzene or naphthalene may be effective if the lids are tightly fitting. One pound of crystals of the particular chemical should be used for each ten cubic feet of space. The young larvae and the beetles are the most easily killed by these chemicals but the containers must be kept tightly closed. Blankets and furnishings treated in this manner should be hung up in a good current of air for ventilation in order that the aromatic odour can be dispersed.

The fully grown larvae of Carpet Beetles (the Woolly Bears) appear to be resistant to modern contact insecticides because they are able to crawl about long after they have come into contact with a lethal dose of insecticide. Perseverance and patience must be exercised in dealing with this pest as immediate results will seldom be achieved.

Cluster Flies and Swarming Flies

There seems to be no method of preventing Cluster Flies from invading premises which they find suitable. They appear to effect an entrance through very small crevices under tiles or round ill-fitting windows. In rooms where there are funishings, a pyrethrum-based fly spray or aerosol may be used, but in roof-spaces or lofts an insecticidal smoke generator is recommended. It is wise to ignite the latter in a bucket on the bottom of which is placed some sand in order to minimize the risk of fire. Before using a spray, it is a valuable suggestion to warm the room in order to increase the activity of the Cluster Flies.

During periods of warm weather the flies are attracted to the windows, and the application of a residual type insecticide by brush around the window frames is efficacious. Another method of eliminating them, easily

L

carried out by the housewife in small rooms, is to suck them into the vacuum cleaner and then to draw into the bag a little Lindane dust and allow a few hours before emptying. In some circumstances, such as high rooms, thatched roofs or very large numbers of flies, it is advisable to contact a servicing company.

Cockroaches

German Cockroaches make only occasional short gliding flights, so that for the purposes of treatment they should be considered as crawling insects. Cockroaches are, however, difficult insects to control, mainly because they are large insects and thus require a larger amount of insecticide to produce lethal effects than for a small insect. In addition they congregate in situations difficult of access to the householder, behind cookers and sinks, behind hot-water pipes and furniture. Under floorboards and in dry conditions generally powder insecticides should be used but on smooth surfaces such as tiles, oil-based sprays are recommended. In the case of a Cockroach infestation, however, the best advice would be to call on the services of a pest control company who may, in some circumstances, apply an insecticidal lacquer.

Earwigs

These insects move only at night so that one method of preventing their entry into houses is to keep windows tightly closed at night or to fit gauze frames. When they effect an entrance they become widely scattered, making their control difficult although they tend to accumulate in more humid places such as the bathroom. Out of doors it is recommended that long grass, herbage and especially creeping plants such as ivy and *Ampelopsis* ('Virginia Creeper)' are removed from within three feet or so of the walls. These cleared areas may be sprayed or dusted with residual-type insecticides and this treatment should be repeated especially during damp weather.

Fleas

Accurate identification is essential and if the fleas are found to be from a cat or a dog then the animal's bedding should be removed and burnt and all accumulations of dirt and debris removed. The animal's usual sleeping place, kennel or basket, should be thoroughly cleaned with hot water. Clean bedding material should then be supplied treated with insecticidal powder specifically formulated for this purpose. Powder should also be dusted into the roots of the hair of the animals. Great care must be taken, however, especially in the case of cats, as they lick themselves and might swallow a quantity of the insecticide, with unfortunate results. Flea larvae will not survive in clean conditions so that all possible nearby breeding sites should have attention paid to them. Dirty floors and carpets, soiled garments lying on the floor, deep cracks in flooring filled with miscellaneous debris and similar situations must be thoroughly cleaned and sprayed, and unclean furnishings and debris ruthlessly burnt. In badly infested rooms a smoke generator of the BHC type is advised.

If a person has to visit flea-infested premises a repellent such as dimethyl-phthalate may be applied to clothing, for example socks, trouser-cuffs and neck-bands, and to the skin also, provided that it does not come into contact with the nose, eyes or mouth.

In the case of the Human Flea, the larvae also cannot exist in scrupulously clean premises, but of course the adults often transfer their attentions at places of entertainment. This usually entails a thorough search for the offender. When a flea is in the bed it may easily be trapped by turning the bedclothes back carefully and dabbing a moistened tablet of soap onto it quickly when it is seen.

Flies

Fly control is best carried out by a combined attack on both the adult flies indoors and the larvae out of doors in their breeding sites. The regular emptying of dustbins or removal of garbage is essential. Manure heaps near the house must be covered with a layer of soil. Indoors, the flies should be sprayed with a 'knockdown' type of insecticide. In addition the treatment of the usual resting places of the flies should be treated with a spray of the residual type. Some flies are resistant to certain chlorinated hydrocarbon insecticides but pest control companies utilize other types such as organo-phosphorus sprays if resistance is encountered.

Ground Beetles

It is seldom that these beetles enter houses in numbers more than two or three at a time, so that they can be ejected out of doors without much trouble. They mostly enter the house by crawling under the doors so that more tightly fitting doors will prevent their ingress. Draught-excluding strip will usually effect this.

Lice

For Head Lice the best treatment is to comb the hair thoroughly with a fine metal comb. Make sure that the comb is always in contact with the skin so that the whole length of each hair is combed. This will remove most of the lice as well as a considerable proportion of the 'nits' (the eggs cemented to the hair). One of the persistent insecticides should then be applied such as 0·2 per cent *gamma* BHC suspension, 2·0 per cent DDT emulsion or Lethane Hair Oil. It would be wise for other members of the family living in the same house to apply the insecticide also. The first two products mentioned are aqueous and the third is oily, and although it possesses an objectionable smell it kills louse eggs, which the other products do not. The hair should not be washed until a week after the treatment when it will be found that the lice are no longer present.

For Body Lice use about an ounce of 5 per cent DDT sprinkled on the inner surface of all the under garments coming into contact with the skin. Pay special attention to all seams.

Mosquitoes

Adult mosquitoes found in the home are best dealt with summarily and directly with a 'knockdown'-type spray. An aerosol is a handy means in such cases.

During summer, if the wriggling larvae are to be seen in water-butts and similar situations, one spot of paraffin or some other light oil will quickly spread over the whole surface of the water and will prevent the mosquito larvae from balancing themselves at the water surface in order to bring about air exchange for their respiration. In the event of very large numbers of mosquitoes (and other noxious flies) entering the house, constituting an invasion from some nearby swampy area, then the best plan would be to inform the public health department of the local authority.

Mites

The Flour Mite

Infested foodstuff should be quickly disposed of by burning. Then ventilate the larder and endeavour to reduce the relative humidity. Foodstuff only lightly infested which it is proposed to eat may be refrigerated, which reduces the mites' activity but does not kill them, or heated above 35° C. (95° F.) which usually kills them if the food is of such a nature that it can be put into an oven for a fairly lengthy period.

The Harvest Mite

The mites may be prevented from attacking the person by the use of repellents: dimethylphthalate or benzyl benzoate applied undiluted to cuffs, around the tops of socks or other openings of the clothes which expose the skin. Such protection is said to last about a fortnight.

The House Mite

As these mites feed on the microscopic superficial growth of mildew which grows on damp walls or on the surface of damp furniture, it is only necessary to dry out the room thoroughly to get rid of them. Essentially the cause of dampness must be removed, then keep good fires going and well ventilate the room. Another method which has been recommended is to close the doors and windows and heat the rooms with fires to as high a temperature as possible.

Scabies Mite

The mites in the skin are killed by an application over the whole body of an acaricidal preparation, such as an emulsion of benzyl benzoate. One application is usually considered to be sufficient but a second is normally advised after two or three days as a safeguard. When all the mites have been killed the general sensitized condition of the skin disappears although isolated areas of irritation may reappear for a few weeks.

The Clover Mite

The best thing that can be done indoors is to remove the mites with a vacuum cleaner. Out of doors it is suggested that a strip of soil about three feet wide is maintained devoid of vegetation all round the house. An official recommendation is given for a thorough drenching of grass and other herbage surrounding the dwelling, as well as around doorways and windows, with an emulsion of 1 per cent Malathion. An emulsion of 1 per cent Lindane is also reported as successfully controlling this troublesome mite.

Moths

Much can be done in the home to *prevent* moth damage occurring. Keep woollen clothes scrupulously clean. Moth damage almost always occurs where food stains or perspiration or urine stains have occurred. After cleaning, woollen clothes should be stored in sealed polythene bags or in tightly closed cupboards protected with such repellents as paradichlorbenzene or naphthalene.

If carpets are cleaned regularly with a vacuum cleaner or carpet sweeper they are unlikely to be damaged by moth grubs except in places covered by heavy furniture, such as a sideboard or piano. These latter situations should be sprayed every six months with a residual type spray. A similar spray should be used around fitted carpets where there is a double thickness of the carpet. It is a very wise precaution to spray the underside of a carpet and around the edge of the floor *before* a carpet is fitted.

Moth larvae cannot exist in bright light and good ventilation, so that it is a good plan to air *regularly* stored blankets, furnishings and other woollen products out of doors on fresh sunny days. Give them a good shaking and brushing or beating, before folding and putting away.

Upholstered furniture is sometimes an important reservoir of moth infestation. The moth larvae may attack in some numbers the inside of the cover where they are, to some extent, protected. They may often provide little evidence of their presence except for an occasional full-fed larva crawling away on the floor, seeking a situation in which to pupate. There is nothing for it but to remove some of the covering from the bottom of the chair and to give a thorough spraying with a residual type insecticide.

Sudden alteration of temperature kills all stages of Clothes Moths and this fact lends point to the cold storage of furs which is usual during the summer months. It must be remembered, however, that cold storage, like heat treatment, which is also sometimes resorted to, does not confer any degree of immunity on the material. As soon as the woollen or fur article returns to ordinary room temperature it is liable to become reinfested if a female moth alights on it and lays some eggs.

Spider Beetles

Make sure that no packet of food material in the larder is acting as a reservoir of infestation by Australian Spider Beetle (which is commonly the case). Other species of Spider Beetle, including Golden Spider Beetle, are able to subsist on miscellaneous debris under skirting-boards and in floor cracks. These locations therefore should be liberally dusted with a residual type powder insecticide and blown and brushed as deeply as possible into the potential breeding-places.

Woodworm

The extermination of infestations in furniture by the two species *Anobium punctatum* and *Lyctus brunneus* is a relatively simple operation provided a few simple rules are followed.

In the first place *all* the wooden surfaces of the article should be treated with the woodworm-killing fluids, making sure at the time of purchase that there are no stipulations on the label that only the unpolished surfaces of the article may be treated. It is best to turn the piece upside-down and start by brushing the fluid with a clean stiff brush into all the corners and crevices. Make sure that all the glue-blocks are treated because these are often of softwood or, in the case of mahogany furniture, of birch. The latter is very susceptable to attack by *A. punctatum*, and yet when it is stained red it is very similar in appearance to mahogany. True mahogany, i.e. timber converted from trees of the genus *Swietenia* growing in the tropical American region, is not attacked by Furniture Beetles.

Do not forget to brush the bottom under-surfaces of the legs of the furniture, i.e. those under-surfaces in actual contact with the floor. When a beetle walks across the floor such surfaces are the first parts of the furniture with which it comes into contact and often it is rough end-grain, a very attractive site for egg-laying.

If the piece of furniture is badly infested with a large number of flight-holes already in evidence then it is a good plan, *in addition* to the overall brush coat, to inject the same fluid into the holes. Often in bad infestations the internal honeycombing is shown up by the fluid emerging from flight-holes at a distance from that into which it is being injected. Of course, it is not necessary to inject every hole; one every four inches or so is quite sufficient.

Sufficient fluid should be applied but there is no sense in brushing on an excess. One good liberal brush coat on softwood with all the surface wetted is a coverage of approximately 200 square feet to the gallon. Rentokil Woodworm Killer should be applied at this rate. The last part of the operation is to apply a brush coat of the fluid over all the polished surfaces. It is true that Furniture Beetle does not lay its eggs on such surfaces but it will do so in joins and cracks on polished surfaces. The product named above does not harm french or cellulose polish but all oil-solvent preparations will remove wax polish so that it is necessary to give the furniture a good wax polish afterwards. Rentokil Wax Polish is ideal for this because it further enhances the insecticidal properties of the treated surfaces and it is a good plan to use this polish or the cream version for the regular periodic polishing.

The treatment outlined above will not only prevent any further disfiguring Furniture Beetle of *Lyctus* flight-holes appearing but, because the preparations are absorbed into the wood, will convey protection against these insects for many years, certainly upwards of twenty years.

It has already been mentioned that woodworm-killing preparations are of the oil-solvent type in order to effect the maximum penetration of the wood and so certain precautions must be taken when using them. Take special care not to get the fluid on to plaster, paper or textiles, or an oily stain will result.

Structural timbers in a house, such as floor joists and flooring, ceiling joists and purlins are very often attacked by *Anobium punctatum*. It is usual in such cases for a servicing firm to carry out the work of eradication and there are special reasons why the effect of the treatment is long lasting so that a long-term guarantee can be given, twenty years being the usual period. If, however, such a large-scale treatment is attempted by the householder the following points should be noted:

1. Just as in the case of furniture, treat *all* surfaces of the woodwork it is possible to reach. This means taking up floorboards but *not* removing slates or tiles.

2. Clean all the wood to be treated preferably by vacuum cleaner and remove debris.

3. Deal with each section separately and thoroughly, keeping a record of which timbers have been treated in case a continuous operation is not possible. *Do not* dash from one patch of flight-holes to another.

4. Do not forget the particularly vulnerable areas—top and bottom edges of doors, top of picture-rail, cupboard under the stairs, supports around water-tank in roof void.

5. Attach all bills for woodworm-killing fluid to household documents. They may well be worth their face value in the future when you or your heirs wish to sell the house.

Household Insect Pests and the Law

To a limited extent society is protected against persons who permit major infestations of insects and mites to proliferate in their homes, by the provisions of Acts of Parliament. If public health is endangered or if a nuisance is created, then a legal liability occurs. Under certain conditions the local authority or the local education committee is empowered to deal with verminous conditions. The word 'verminous' has two meanings entomologically: a verminous building implies infestation by Bed Bugs, and/or fleas, whereas a verminous person implies infestation by lice or Scabies Mite.

Under the Public Health Act (1936) and the closely parallel Public Health (London) Act (1936), a Medical Officer of Health or a Sanitary Inspector (now called a Public Health Inspector) may report the existence of verminous conditions to the Local Authority who are then empowered to act in several ways, as follows:

1. They may destroy or clean verminous articles, and whilst provision is made for compensation, cost of cleaning is borne by the Local Authority.

2. They may serve notice to the owner of the verminous house to have it disinfested at his own expense. In default the local Authority may have this carried out and recover the cost from the owner. There is one exception to this: if fumigation by hydrogen cyanide gas is recommended in the report of the Medical Officer of Health then this is carried out at public expense.

3. They may set up 'Cleansing Stations' for the disinfestation of articles and persons. A verminous person may be forced by Order of the Court to be disinfested.

Under the Education Act (1944) (and to a limited extent covered by the Public Health (London) Act (1936)) a County Medical Officer of Health, or a person acting for him, is empowered to inspect school-children in schools of Local Education Authorities, for verminous condition. If such is found they will require the parents or guardians to disinfest the child within twenty-four hours, in their own home, in default of which the child may be disinfested at the 'Cleansing Station' set up by the Local Authority.

Under the Scabies Order, 1941, which was an Order in Council under the Emergency Powers (Defence) Regulations, the Local Authority is empowered to inspect houses which they have reasonable grounds for belief are inhabited or have recently been inhabited by verminous persons. This order, therefore, although referring only to Scabies in the title, is applicable also to infestation by lice. Any person living in the house may be required to attend a medical examination and if necessary to undergo treatment or disinfestation.

The Prevention of Damage by Pests Act (1949) did not involve dwellings in the ordinary sense, its main object being to enforce notification by persons concerned in the manufacture, transport, storage and sale of food, of infestations by rodents, insects and mites. However, the Public Health Act (1936) which has already been referred to, gave definitions of statutory nuisances involving verminous buildings and accumulations of manure or refuse in which flies and other insects were breeding and invading nearby properties.

It is noteworthy that Local Authorities, who had the power to initiate proceedings against the owners of such buildings constituting a nuisance or 'being in such a state as to be prejudicial to health', use these powers to a decreasing extent. This is due both to large-scale rehousing in recent years and to great improvement in standards of hygiene brought about by education. It is of interest to note that Local Authorities have used the presence of widespread woodworm damage as the reason for taking action against a landlord because the state of the flooring was 'prejudicial to health'. Presumably the tenant was in danger of breaking a limb if the floor gave away!

BIBLIOGRAPHY

ANON. *Lice*. British Museum (Natural History) Economic Series 2a (1954).

BUSVINE, J. *Insects and Hygiene*. Methuen, London (1951).

CLOUDSLEY-THOMPSON, J. L. *Spiders, Scorpions, Centipedes and Mites*. Pergamon Press, London (1958).

CLOUDSLEY-THOMPSON, J. L. and SANKEY, J. *Land Invertebrates*. Methuen, London (1961).

EVANS, O. E. and BROWNING, E. *Some British Mites of Economic Importance*. British Museum (N.H.), Economic Series No. 17 (1955).

COLYER, C. N. and HAMMOND, C. O. *Flies of the British Isles*. Warne, London (1961).

PAPWORTH, D. S. Practical Experience with the Control of Ants in Britain. *Ann. appl. Biol.* **46,** 106–11 (1958).

PARKIN, E. A. Some Insect Invaders of Domestic Premises. *Ann. appl. Biol.* **46,** 120–1 (1958).

PEACOCK, A. D., HALL, D. W., SMITH, I. C. and GOODFELLOW, A. *The Biology and Control of the Ant Pest*. H.M.S.O. Miscellaneous Publication No. 17 (1950).

SMIT., F. G. A. M. Handbooks for the Identification of British Insects. Siphonaptera. *R. ent. Soc. Lond.* **1,** pt. 16 (1957).

SOLOMON, M. E. Ecology of the Flour Mite, *Acarus siro* L. *Ann. appl. Biol.* **50,** 178–84. (1962).

SOLOMON, M. E Mites in Houses, Shops and other Occupied Buildings. *The Sanitarian*. March 1961 (1961).

TYLER, P. S. Cluster Flies and Swarming Flies; Their Behaviour and Control. *The Sanitarian* (1961).

Index

Acarus siro, 14, 19, 142, 143
  appearance of, 142
  control of, 160
  economic importance of, 143
  life-cycle of, 143
Adalia bipunctata, 98, 99
Adalia decempunctata, 99
Aedes caspius, 131
Aerosol insecticides, 155, 156
Alimentary canal of insects, 22–4
Allolobophora chlorotica, 113, 114
Anisopus fenestralis, 14, 115, 116
  appearance of, 115
  economic importance of, 116
  life-cycle of, 115, 116
Anobium punctatum, 10, 13, 19, 75–8
  appearance of, 75, 76, 83
  control of, 162, 163
  economic importance of, 77, 78
  life-cycle of, 76, 77
  parasites and predators of, 78, 79
  reproductive system of, 29
Anopheles atroparvus, 14, 129
Anopheles maculipennis, 14, 18, 128, 129
Anopheline mosquitoes, 126–31
  appearance of, 126
  diseases carried by, 126
  economic importance of, 131
  life-cycle of, 126–8
  species of, 129
Anthrenus verbasci, 13, 19, 93–6
  appearance of, 93, 95
  economic importance of, 95, 96
  life-cycle of, 94, 95
Ants as household pests, 38, 109–12
  control of, 156
Arachnida, characteristics of the, 18
Armadillidium vulgare, 14, 138
Arthropoda, classification of the, 17–20]
Attagenus pellio, 13, 19, 96–8
  appearance of, 96
  economic importance of, 97, 98
  life-cycle of, 96, 97
Attagenus piceus, 96–98
  appearance of, 96
  economic importance of, 97, 98
  life-cycle of, 96, 97
Australian Spider Beetle, the, see
  Ptinus tectus

Bacon Beetle, the, see *Dermestes
  lardarius*
Bed Bug, the, see *Cimex lectularius*
Beetles as household pests, 75–104
Bird Lice, see Biting Lice
Biscuit Beetle, the, see *Stegobium
  paniceum*
Biting Lice, 37, 58, 59
Black Beetle, the, see *Blatta orientalis*
Black Carpet Beetle, the, see *Attagenus
  piceus*
Black Garden Ant, the, see *Lasius
  (Acanthomyops) niger*
Blatta orientalis, 9, 13, 19, 37, 47–50
  alimentary canal of, 22, 23
  appearance of, 31–3, 47
  control of, 158
  economic importance of, 50
  life-cycle of, 47–50
  nervous system of, 24, 25
  reproductive system of, 28, 29
Blattella germanica, 13, 19, 37, 50–2
  appearance of, 50
  control of, 158
  economic importance of, 52
  life-cycle of, 50–2
Blood system of insects, 21, 22
Blowflies, the, 120–2
Blue Bottles, the, 120–2
Body Louse, the, see *Pediculus humanus*
  var. *corporis*
Book Lice, 37, 56, 57
Bread Beetle, the, see *Stegobium
  paniceum*
Bristletails, the, see *Lepisma
  saccharina*
Brown House Moth, the,
  see *Hofmannophila pseudospretella*
Bryobia praetiosa, 14, 20, 147, 148
  appearance of, 148
  control of, 161
  economic importance of, 148
  life-cycle of, 148

Calliphora erythrocephala, 14, 120–2
  appearance of, 120, 121
  economic importance of, 122
  life-cycle of 121, 122, 120–2

Calliphora vomitoria, 120–2
  appearance of, 120
  economic importance of, 122
  life-cycle of, 121, 122
Campodeiform larvae, 35
Carpet Beetles, the, 9, 10, 71, 91–8
  control of, 157
Case-Bearing Clothes Moth, see *Tinaea pellionella*
Castor Bean Tick, the, see *Ixodes ricinus*
Cat Flea, the, see *Ctenocephalides felis*
Centipedes as household pests, 139, 140
Chilopoda, characteristics of the, 18
Chrysopa carnea, 13, 20, 67
  appearance of, 67
  economic importance of, 67
  life-cycle of, 67
Cimex lectularius, 9, 10, 13, 18, 37, 64–6
  appearance of, 64
  control of, 156, 157
  economic importance of, 65, 66
  life-cycle of, 33, 64, 65
Classification of insects, 36–9
Clothes moths, the, 9, 10, 19, 68–72
  control of, 161, 162
  classification of, 69
  origin of wool feeding habit, 68, 69
  parasites and predators of, 74
Clover Mite, the, see *Bryobia praetiosa*
Cluster Fly, the, see *Pollenia rudis*
Coccinella septempunctata, 99
Cockroach, the, see *Blatta orientalis*
Coelopa frigida, 14, 122
  appearance of, 122
  economic importance of, 122
  life-cycle of, 122
Common Clothes Moth, the,
  see *Tineola bisselliella*
Common Cockroach, the,
  see *Blatta orientalis*
Common Furniture Beetle, the,
  see *Anobium punctatum*
Common Gnat, the, see *Culex pipiens*
Common House Fly, the, see *Musca domestica*
Common Sheep Tick, the, see *Ixodes ricinus*
Common Wasp, the, see *Paravespula vulgaris*
Coninomus nodifer, 14, 101–4
Coniophora cerebella, 84, 89
Control of insect pests, 153–65
  choice of insecticides for, 153–5
  laws for, 163–5
Crab Louse, the, see *Phthirus pubis*
Crane-Flies, the, 14, 122, 125, 126
  appearance of, 122, 125, 126
  economic importance of, 126
  life-cycle of, 126
Crustacea, characteristics of the, 17
Cryptophagus acutangulus, 14, 101–4
Cryptophagus cellaris, 14, 101–4
Cryptophagus distinguendus, 14, 101–4

Ctenocephalides canis, 14, 132–6
  appearance of, 132, 133
  control of, 158, 159
  economic importance of, 136
  life-cycle of, 134–6
Ctenocephalides felis, 14, 132–6
  appearance of, 132, 133, 135
  control of, 158, 159
  economic importance of, 136
  life-cycle of, 134–6
Culex molestus, 131
Culex pipiens, 14, 131
Culicine mosquitoes, 126–31
  appearance of, 126
  diseases carried by, 126
  economic importance of, 131
  life-cycle of, 126, 127
  species of, 128, 130, 131

Daddy-Long-Legs, see Crane Flies
Dasyphora cyanella, 14, 124
  appearance of, 124
  economic importance of, 124
  life-cycle of, 124
Death Watch Beetle, the, see
  Xestobium rufovillosum
Dermestes lardarius, 13, 19, 92, 93
  appearance of, 92
  economic importance of, 93
  life-cycle of, 92, 93
Dermestes maculatus, 92
Diplopoda, characteristics of the, 18
Dipylidium caninum, 63, 136
Disease
  ants as carriers of, 111
  fleas as carriers of, 132, 136
  flies as carriers of, 113, 120
  Fur Beetle as carrier of, 98
  mites as carriers of, 147
  ticks as carriers of, 150
Dog Biting Louse, the, see *Trichodectes canis*
Dog Flea, the, see *Ctenocephalides canis*
Dog Sucking Louse, the,
  see *Linognathus setosus*
Drosophila fasciata, 124
Drosophila fenestrarum, 124
Drosophila funebris, 124
Drosophila melanogaster, 123
Drosophila obscura, 124
Drosophila repleta, 123, 124
Drosophila spp., 4, 122–4
  appearance of, 123
  economic importance of, 124
  life-cycle of, 124
Drug Store Beetle, the,
  see *Stegobium paniceum*
Dry Rot fungus, see *Merulius lacrymans*

Earwig, the, see *Forficula auricularia*
Education Act (1944), 164
Emergency Powers (Defence)
  Regulations (1941), 164

Endopterygotous insects, 35
Endrosis sarcitrella, 13, 74
  appearance of, 74
  economic importance of, 74
  life-cycle of, 74
Enicmus minutus, 101–4
Euophryum confine, 13, 80–2, 104
  appearance of, 80, 81
  economic importance of, 82
  life-cycle of, 81, 82
Evolution of insects, 36
Exopterygotous insects, 34
Exoskeleton of insects, 30, 31

Fannia canicularis, 14, 18, 118–20
  appearance of, 118, 119
  economic importance of, 119, 120
  life-cycle of, 119
Firebrat, the, see *Thermobia domestica*
Fleas as household pests, 38, 132–6
  control of, 158, 159
Flesh Fly, the, see *Sarcophaga carnaria*
Flies as household pests, 38, 113–31
  control of, 157–9
Flour Mite, the, see *Acarus siro*
Forficula auricularia, 13, 37, 53–5
  appearance of, 54
  control of, 158
  economic importance of, 55
  life-cycle of, 54, 55
Fruit-Flies, see *Drosophila* spp.
Fungus Beetles, see Plaster Beetles
Fur Beetle, the, see *Attagenus pellio*
Furniture Beetle, see *Anobium puctatum*
Furniture Mite, the, see *Glycyphagus domesticus*

Garden Weevil, the, see *Otiorrhynchus rugostriatus*
German Cockroach, the, see *Blattella germanica*
Gibbium psylloides, 13, 91
  appearance of, 91
  economic importance of, 91
  life-cycle of, 91
Glycyphagus domesticus, 14, 141, 142
  appearance of, 141
  control of, 160
  economic importance of, 142
  life-cycle of, 141, 142
Golden Spider Beetle, the, see *Niptus hololeucus*
Gooseberry Mite, the, see *Bryobia praetiosa*
Grain Itch Mite, the, see *Pyemotes (Pediculoides) ventricosus*
Green Bottles, the, 120–2
Green Cluster Fly, the, see *Dasyphora cyanella*
Green Lacewing, the, see *Chrysopa carnea*
Ground Beetles, 13, 99, 100
  appearance of, 99, 100

control of, 159
economic importance of, 100
life-cycle of, 100
Growth of insects, 35, 36
Gryllulus domesticus, 13, 19, 52, 53
  appearance of, 52, 53
  economic importance of, 53
  life-cycle of, 53

Harpalus rufipes, 99, 100
Harvest Mite, the, see *Trombicula autumnalis*
Head Louse, the, see *Pediculus humanus* var. *capitis*
Heterometabolous insects, 34
Hide Beetles, the, 91–98
Hofmannophila pseudospretella, 19, 73, 74
  appearance of, 73
  economic importance of, 73, 74
  life-cycle of, 34, 35, 73
Holometabolous insects, 34, 35
Honey-Bee, the, 9, 105
House Cricket, the, see *Gryllulus domesticus*
House Longhorn Beetle, the, see *Hylotrupes bajulus*
House Mite, the, see *Glycyphagus domesticus*
House Moths, 19, 73, 74
  classification of, 69
  origin of wool feeding habit, 68, 69
  parasites and predators of, 74
Human Flea, the, see *Pulex irritans*
Human Louse, the, see *Pediculus humanus* (var. *capitis* and *corporis*)
Hump Spider Beetle, the, see *Gibbium psylloides*
Hylotrupes bajulus, 13, 82, 83
  appearance of, 82
  economic importance of, 83
  life-cycle of, 82, 83

Insect orders, 36–8
Insecticides,
  choice of, 153–5
  hazards connected with, 155
Insects,
  anatomy of, 21–33
  characteristics of, 17
  classification of, 36–9
  distribution of, 18–20
  evolution of, 36
  growth of, 35, 36
  life-cycle of, 33–5
  nature of, 17–20
Itch Mite, the, see *Sarcoptes scabiei*
Ixodes ricinus, 14, 149, 150
  appearance of, 149, 150
  economic importance of, 150
  life-cycle of, 149

'Knockdown' insecticides, 153, 154
Korynetes caeruleus, 78

Lacewing Fly, the, see *Chrysopa carnea*
Lacewings as household pests, 38, 67
Ladybird Beetles, 13, 19, 100, 101
    appearance of, 87, 100
    economic importance of, 101
    life-cycle of, 100, 101
Larder Beetle, the, see *Dermestes lardarius*
Lasius (*Acanthomyops*) *niger*, 14, 19, 111, 112
    appearance of, 111, 112
    economic importance of, 112
    life-cycle of, 112
Lathridius bergrothi, 14, 101–4
Lathridius nodifer, 101–4
Laws controlling insect pests, 163–5
Leather Jackets, the, see Crane Flies
Lepisma saccharina, 13, 36, 43, 44
    appearance of, 32, 43
    economic importance of, 43, 44
    life-cycle of, 44
Lesser House Fly, the, see *Fannia canicularis*
Lice as household pests, 56–63
    control of, 159, 160
Life-cycle of insects, 33–5
Linnaean system, 39
Linnaeus, 39
Linognathus setosus, 13, 63
    appearance of, 63
    life-cycle of, 63
Liposcelis divinatorius, 13, 56, 57
    appearance of, 56
    economic importance of, 57
    life-cycle of, 56, 57
Lithobius forficatus, 14, 140
Lucilia caesar, 120–2
Lucilia sericata, 121, 122
Lyctus brunneus, 10, 13, 19, 86–8
    appearance of, 86, 87
    control of, 162, 163
    economic importance of, 88
    life-cycle of, 87, 88

Mahogany Flats, see *Cimex lectularius*
Mealworm Beetle, the, see *Tenebrio molitor*
Merulius lacrymans, 86, 103
Mites as household pests, 18, 141–9
    control of, 160, 161
Monomorium pharaonis, 14, 19, 109–11
    appearance of, 109, 110
    economic importance of, 110, 111
    life-cycle of, 110
Mosquitoes as household pests, 126–31
    control of, 160
Moths as household pests, 38, 68–74
    control of, 161, 162
Musca domestica, 14, 18, 117, 118
    appearance of, 116, 117
    economic importance of, 118
    life-cycle of, 117, 118

Nacerdes melanura, 13, 85, 86
    appearance of, 85, 86
    economic importance of, 86
    life-cycle of, 86
Names of insects, 39
Necrophlaeophagus longicornis, 140
Nervous system of insects, 22, 24–6
Niptus hololeucus, 13, 90, 91
    appearance of, 90
    control of, 162
    economic importance of, 91
    life-cycle of, 90, 91

Oak Longhorn Beetle, the, see *Phymatodes testaceus*
Oniscus asellus, 14, 19, 138
Oriental Cockroach, the, see *Blatta orientalis*
Otiorrhynchus rugostriatus, 14, 104
Otiorrhynchus sulcatus, 14, 104

Paravespula germanica, 14, 105–9
    appearance of, 105–7
    economic importance of, 108
    life-cycle of, 107, 108
    sting of, 108, 109
Paravespula vulgaris, 14, 105–9
    appearance of, 105, 106
    economic importance of, 108
    life-cycle of, 107, 108
    sting of, 108, 109
Parthenogenesis, definition of, 29
Pediculus humanus, var. *capitis*, 10, 13, 59, 60
    appearance of, 59
    control of, 159
    economic importance of, 60
    life-cycle of, 60
Pediculus humanus var. *corporis*, 9, 13, 18, 60–2
    appearance of, 60, 61
    control of, 160
    economic importance of, 61, 62
    life-cycle of, 60, 61
Pentarthrum huttoni, 13, 80–2
    see also *Euophryum confine*
Pharaoh's Ant, see *Monomorium pharaonis*
Phthirus pubis, 59, 62, 63
    appearance of, 62
    economic importance of, 62, 63
    life-cycle of, 62
Phymatodes testaceus, 86
Plaster Beetles, 14, 101–4
    appearance of, 102, 103
    economic importance of, 103, 104
    life-cycle of, 103
Pollenia rudis, 14, 113, 114
    appearance of, 113
    control of, 157, 158
    economic importance of, 114
    life-cycle of, 113, 114
Polyembryony, definition of, 29

Porcellio scaber, 14, 138
Powder Post Beetle, the, see *Lyctus brunneus*
Prevention of Damages by Pests Act (1949), 164
Psocids, see Book Lice
Ptinus tectus, 13, 19, 89, 90
  appearance of, 89
  control of, 162
  economic importance of, 90
  life-cycle of, 90
Pubic Louse, the, see *Phthirus pubis*
Public Health Act (1936), 164
Public Health (London) Act (1936), 164
Pulex irritans, 14, 18, 132-6
  appearance of, 132-4
  control of, 159
  economic importance of, 136
  life-cycle of, 134-6
Pyemotes (Pediculoides) ventricosus, 14, 78, 148, 149
  appearance of, 148, 149
  economic importance of, 148

Rat Flea, the, see *Xenopsylla cheopis*
Reproductive system of insects, 28-30
Residual insecticides, 153, 154
Respiratory system of insects, 26, 27
Rhagonycha fulva, 86

Sarcophaga carnaria, 120
Sarcoptes scabiei, 14, 18, 143-5
  appearance of, 143, 144
  control of, 160, 161
  economic importance of, 145
  life-cycle of, 144, 145
Scabies Mite, the, see *Sarcoptes scabiei*
Scabies Order (1941), 164
Scarabaeiform larvae, 35
Scenopinus fenestralis, 74
Seaweed Fly, the, see *Coelopa frigida*
Shape of insects, 31-3
Shiner, the, see *Blattella germanica*
Short-nosed Weevils, the, 104
Silverfish, the, see *Lepisma saccharina*
Skeletal system of insects, 29-31
Small Tortoiseshell Butterfly, the, 19
Social Survey of the Central Office of Information, 71
Spathius exarator, 74
Spider Beetles, the, see *Ptinus tectus* and *Niptus hololeucus*
Springtails, the, 37, 46
Steamfly, the, see *Blattella germanica*
Stegobium paniceum, 13, 19, 86, 87
  appearance of, 87
  economic importance of, 87
  life-cycle of, 87
Strawberry Seed Beetle, the, see *Harpalus rufipes*
Sucking Lice, the, 37, 57, 59-63

Taeniorhynchus richiardii, 14, 129-31
Tapestry Moth, the, see *Trichophaga tapetzella*
Tenebrio molitor, 13, 87-9
  appearance of, 88
  economic importance of, 89
  life-cycle of, 88, 89
Tenebrio obscurus, 88
Thaumatomyia notata, 14, 116
  appearance of, 116
  economic importance of, 116
  life-cycle of, 116
Theobaldia annulata, 14, 130, 131
Theocolax formiciformis, 78
Thermobia domestica, 13, 44-6
  appearance of, 44, 45
  economic importance of, 45
  life-cycle of, 45, 46
Ticks as household pests, 18, 141, 149, 150
Tinaea pellionella, 13, 71, 72
  appearance of, 71
  economic importance of, 72
  life-cycle of 72
Tineola bisselliella, 13, 19, 38, 69-71
  appearance of, 69
  economic importance of, 71
  life-cycle of, 69-71
Tipula paludosa, 125
Trichodectes canis, 13, 57-9
  appearance of, 58
  economic importance of, 58, 59
  life-cycle of, 58
Trichophaga tapetzella, 13, 72
  appearance of, 72
  economic importance of, 72
  life-cycle of, 72
Trogium pulsatorium, 56
Trombicula autumnalis, 14, 145-7
  appearance of, 145, 146
  control of, 160
  economic importance of, 146, 147
  life-cycle of, 145, 146
Tyroglyphus farinae, see *Acarus siro*

Varied Carpet Beetle, the, see *Anthrenus verbasci*
Vascular system of insects, 21, 22
Vinegar Flies, see *Drosophila* spp.

Wasps as household pests, 38, 105-9
Wharf Borer, the, see *Nacerdes melanura*
White-Shouldered House Moth, the, see *Endrosis sarcitrella*
White-Tip Clothes Moth, the, see *Trichophaga tapetzella*
Window Gnat, the, see *Anisopus fenestralis*
Wine Flies, 122, 123
Wood-boring Beetles, the, 75-80
Wood-boring Weevils, the, 80-2, 104

Wood Lice, the, 17, 137, 138
  appearance of, 138
Woodworm, see *Anobium punctatum*
  and *Lyctus brunneus*
Woolly Bears, the, 157

Xenopsylla cheopis, 136

Xestobium rufovillosum, 13, 79, 80
  appearance of, 79, 83
  economic importance of, 80
  life-cycle of, 79, 80

Yellow Swarming Fly, the, see
  Thaumatomyia notata